IN THE NAME OF SANITY

BOOKS BY LEWIS MUMFORD

In the Name of Sanity

of Sanity

BY LEWIS MUMFORD

HARCOURT, BRACE AND COMPANY   NEW YORK

LIBRARY OF CONGRESS CATALOG CARD NUMBER: 54-11324

PRINTED IN THE UNITED STATES OF AMERICA

BY THE HADDON CRAFTSMEN, INC., SCRANTON, PA.

 1

The aim of this book is to give fresh insight—and with that insight hope and courage—to those who are disquieted by the violence and irrationality of our times. Most of the chapters were originally presented as lectures; so there lingers in their prose the rhythms, and perhaps occasionally the repetitions, of oral discourse. I shall not apologize for these qualities if, at the same time, they evoke, as an effective lecture does, a continuous dialogue between the speaker and the audience. For it is not to present a ready-made solution to the problems of our time, but to suggest an attitude and a philosophy capable of meeting them that I have put these thoughts together.

CONTENTS

IN THE NAME OF SANITY

I

IN THE NAME OF SANITY

Until sanity reawakens among the "tribes and nations and kindreds," the threat of a final apocalypse of violence will continue to hover over mankind. The only purpose of such a war of extermination—a war that would, at the very least, liquidate civilization—would be to relieve by action the irrational terrors and antagonisms that have brought it about. At the end of such a conflict, the savage remnants of the same peoples would face each other, and infinitely worse problems would remain to be settled. But the courage and the hope and the good will that might have been invoked to keep such a war from starting would no longer be available to bring about peace.

If this is a sober estimate of probabilities, it is plain that we are now facing something even worse than war: we are threatened with an outbreak of compulsive irrationality. By reason of the fears and suspicions and hatreds that have been introduced into the affairs of nations during the last four decades, no small part of mankind lives in a state of self-enclosed delusion that calls for psychiatric treatment. Men must recover the capacity for balanced judgment before they can halt the approaching catastrophe and bring about the conditions for peace.

When one speaks of the present state of mankind, one should refer, not to distant enemies and obscure masses of men, but first of all to one's countrymen and oneself. Each of us is in some degree the victim of obsessive prejudices, fixed ideas, narrowed horizons, which limit our contacts with reality and prevent us from appraising fairly the motives and aims of other men. Like their counterparts in Soviet Russia and China, our own leaders are now living in a one-dimensional world of the immediate present, unable to remember the lessons of the past or to anticipate the probabilities of the future: to guarantee national security they have created a state of total insecurity, and in the effort to insure national survival they have perfected weapons whose full-scale use would imperil the future of the human race.

If mankind is not to take the last step into the abyss, we must awaken ourselves from this nightmare, and cleanse ourselves of our present irrationality. In those countries like the United States and England, where men are not yet wholly imprisoned in an official ideology, the obligation to use that freedom is a command. Ap-

plied at the right moment, rationality may prove as in-
fectious as madness.

In a breakdown of sane judgment as general as the
present one, there are no physicians mankind can turn
to for treatment. If light comes it will be through self-
help; by vigils and self-examinations that may terminate
in acts of grace that have heretofore been inconceivable;
and in those preparatory efforts each of us has a part
to play. Our first obligation is the restoration of our
own capacity to be human: to think and feel as whole
men, not as specialists, not as ideologists, not as parti-
sans and experts, not as political or religious sectarians,
not as tribalists and nationalists, but as exponents of
what is veritably human.

Each of us must accept, as his own, the personal responsibility for safeguarding man's essential humanity.
Each of us must challenge the automatisms we have
submitted to and evaluate both the near and the remote
consequences of the forces that we have helped to set
in motion. Above all, we must conquer our moral numbness and inertia: the state that since 1945 has enabled
us, in America, to accept the indiscriminate extermination of human life, by atomic and bacterial means, as
the conceivable act of a sane government engaged in
war. We must uphold love and reason as more precious
than life itself. Rational men can triumph even over

defeat; but the irrational are defeated even by their triumphs: indeed, especially by their triumphs.

One clear act of sanity remains to be performed: to call upon the right reason of our opposite numbers all over the world, in the conviction that mankind as a whole has a repository of sanity and good will that is capable of delivering the race from psychotic malice and irrational violence. This is not an appeal for last-moment conversations "at the highest levels" to halt the present march to war. What the situation demands now is just the opposite: *conversations at the lowest levels:* not a final meeting of the few but a preliminary meeting and joining of the many.

The voices of reason must declare themselves first in private chambers all over the world, even behind Iron Curtains and Chinese Walls: then rise in the quiet exchanges of friend with friend, of workfellow with workfellow, until they swell into a confident public command: "Men and brothers, let us come to our senses and behave like men!" For there is no valid human goal, neither freedom nor solidarity, neither capitalism nor communism, that will not be obliterated in the total madness that will be the fruit of total war.

At this critical moment, we say, only the residual sanity of mankind can rescue the race from the obsessions and compulsions, the fixed ideas and delusional

6

projections, that are paving the way to total disintegration. The chief enemy of peace is the spirit of unreason itself: an inability to conceive alternatives, an unwillingness to reconsider old prejudices, to part with ideological obsessions, to entertain new ideas or to improvise new plans. To us in America, the spirit of unreason shows itself most threateningly in the conduct of the Russian and Chinese governments rejecting every counsel of moderation, deliberately fanning smoldering resentments and envies into flames of active hatred. But that formidable state has its provocative counterparts everywhere: not least in the United States, where reason is cowed by governmental purges and subverted by irrational measures for counteracting subversion; where criticism and dissent and even normal human error are identified as treason; where collective fear is magnified by the very weapons of frightfulness we ourselves have voluminously been producing.

The apostles of reason will unite and point out the most basic fact of all: that neither totalitarianism nor democracy would emerge from a war of total extermination as a victor. The chances are, rather, that neither would emerge at all, except in such demoralized and distorted form as to undermine all that was humanly good in either system. No peace would be possible after such crippling violence, such unappeasable horrors, such

7

bestial dehumanization as would characterize this far-spreading catastrophe: the faith of mankind in its own basic humanity would be undermined for centuries by its creation of a worldwide Auschwitz.

Immanuel Kant said that nothing was unconditionally good except the will to goodness. In a similar vein, one might say that the only sane proposal that remains to be made to mankind today is the proposal to preserve its sanity: to avoid, by a spontaneous upsurge of human purpose, the final horror that automatic thinking in science and technology and politics has actually prepared for us. If we are capable of this first act of reason, we will then follow it through by assiduous demonstrations of good will. We will make our new attitude visible in magnanimity of aim, in generosity of spirit, in patience and forbearance, freeing ourselves from suspicion, hatred and aggression in cumulative acts of love and peace. We shall not forget Gandhi's dictum: "If you want to convert your opponent you must present to him his better and nobler side. . . . Do not dangle his faults before him." Every positive act of love— offering food to hungry peoples, medical aid to the sick, friendly appreciation to the creative gifts of other nations and respect to their individuality—erects a barrier against violence.

Is this a dream? Naturally, it is a dream, for all challenges to animal lethargy and inertia begin in a dream. The dream of flight eventually produced the airplane, and the dream of brotherhood will bring forth, as its engine, an effective world government. But it is better to sink one's last hopes in such a dream than to be destroyed by a nightmare. Only those who can still dream will dare to be human; and only those who dare to be human, with the saving remnant of their reason, will have the audacity to rescue mankind from the compulsions and irrationalities that now undermine our whole civilization.

II

ASSUMPTIONS AND PREDICTIONS

Written in the autumn of 1946, this essay serves as passport and letter of credit for the rest of the volume; for it was conceived and published before the cold war had broken out, before security investigations had been instituted throughout the American government, in short, before the now familiar phenomena described herein had made their appearance. Except for the removal of a single verbal repetition, not a word has been altered.

The social effects of atomic war cannot be dealt with outside space and time: where, when, and how the war takes place will condition the purely physical results and their social consequences. Hence no single projection of a curve that represents the present known factors will suffice. For the sake of reducing the problem to manageable proportions I shall take two constants: the atom bomb itself and a state of chronic non-cooperation between the political powers. On this basis, I shall make a series of alternative assumptions as to the time, the duration, and the destructiveness of the atomic war itself.

First Assumption: The atom bomb is used by the United States against a single power before any other power has an equivalent means of retaliation.

As soon as one makes this assumption, one also lays down certain other conditions. One of them is that the object of such an attack would be Soviet Russia and that the purpose of it would be to safeguard the United States from an unwelcome surprise of a similar nature. On this assumption the Lilienthal plan for safeguarding the production of atomic energy has not yet been put into effect: fear has therefore risen that Russia has been stalling for time and perhaps will soon be at the point of being able to meet our challenge of atomic supremacy halfway.

Unfortunately, the success of such a preventive war depends upon the military element of surprise: hence the assumption of an undeclared war must also be made, which means that the military forces have taken it upon themselves—as part of their "sacred trust" of safeguarding their country from attack—to make the political decision, possibly with the advice and consent of the President, but not with the open authority of the Congress. The necessity for secrecy finds additional justification in the fact that, no matter how steadily political

11

relations between the two countries might deteriorate, it is unlikely that such an attack would have sufficient popular support in advance to sanction a cold-blooded declaration of atomic war. After the attack has taken place, the proofs of its "necessity" can be easily brought to light: the "finding" of an atom bomb, supposedly planted by the enemy, in the heart of Washington or New York; or the reported encountering of an imaginary fleet of Russian bombers, halfway across the Atlantic, as the first strike against the enemy is made.

By hypothesis, the first act of this atomic war is unbelievably successful: every plane finds its target and every bomb reaches it; so that some 36 Russian cities with populations of over 200,000 each are wiped out, in all about 18,000,000 people; and the obliteration of certain other strategic cities of smaller dimensions, removes another 7,000,000: 25,000,000 persons in all. The first newspaper headlines to herald this unprecedented success would undoubtedly read: "Red Menace Removed Forever!" But the elation of victory is presently succeeded by a sense of frustration: for, assuming the present deployment of Russia's military forces, the atomic victory is not at once followed by an unconditional surrender. The United States has done its worst; but it has not yet done enough. Though theoretically wiped out, the Russian Government proceeds to make an effective response to the situation by moving its armies in force to the periphery of Europe and Asia, taking these areas under its protection and summoning them to unite against this Yankee imperialism which has butchered twenty-five million innocent people and plainly is bent on bringing the whole world under its barbarous dominion.

Russia's response takes time; but the fact that Russia's major cities all have been wiped out does not prevent this response from taking place; nor does the wiping out of Russia's military potential prevent her from falling back upon industrial Asia and Europe to serve as arsenal. So, far from the menace of Russian domination being settled, the whole case has in fact become more difficult. Just as in the past the drying up of the grasslands pushed the Mongols and the Huns onto the periphery of the continents, so the radioactivity in the destroyed areas, and the fear of further attacks, set in motion a great mass migration. Though millions will perish on that trek, millions more will reach their destination and mingle with the non-Russian population. Even if the supply of atom bombs is inexhaustible, there is no military answer to this situation. Shall further instruments of extermination then be used to back up the atom bomb? Bacterial warfare perhaps? Not if we hope to follow up our victory anywhere in Eurasia. The large-scale use of a DDT or the spraying of radioactive materials on the land might lead to unparalleled starvation within the Russian domain; but the impulse to adopt these grisly methods must take account of another fact: the growing moral recoil.

In spite of a complete suppression of free discussion over the origins and justifications of this war, in the newspapers and on the radio, a steadily deepening moral reaction has taken place: the very unwillingness of the President and the military authorities to submit to any examination of their case, only increases the general sense of suspicion and guilt. The usual justifications for suppression in wartime are now lacking, for, according to the propaganda issued by the military, the enemy has been wiped out, and the war is all but over. Suspicion and misapprehension grow, however, when an act is presently passed to raise an armed force of ten million amphibious and airborne soldiers for the invasion of Europe and Asia. Even those who had joyfully accepted the atomic victory pause at this next step. Instead of a cheap war, the one-sided atomic war has turned out to be a costly one: instead of a swift war, it promises to have no termination at all. In a country with the territory and population of Russia, even wholesale extermination is still not total extermination. To complete the illusory quality of this victory, and to give it an extra touch of irony, the danger of atomic retaliation has not altogether been removed, for Russia can now look to the willing aid of European and Asiatic scientists: so the main purpose of the attack is, in this event, nullified. Meanwhile, so many links in the process of human co-operation and human understanding would have been destroyed by the very manner in which the attack was carried out, that any hope of bringing about peace and order for centuries would be fantastic.

Second Assumption: War itself does not break out until each of the two chief powers, the United States and Russia, possesses a large stockpile of atom bombs, and by hypothesis, the stockpile of the United States is many times that of Russia.

By the time this war breaks out, certain precautions against surprise have already been taken: every package and crate of goods in international trade is rigorously inspected, not only for radioactive materials but for other mechanical components of the atom bomb, and all direct air travel between continents has broken down: the outlying islands have become halfway stations, and any foreign plane found beyond these points is shot down on sight without warning. Nonintercourse between countries has reached the point where even diplomatic relations between Russia and the United States have been broken, because of the suspicion on each side that the conventions of diplomacy are only a thin disguise for an espionage organization. After a succession of feints and withdrawals, war breaks out on both sides, with or without an accompanying public declaration; for by now the impossibility of publicly declaring war in advance has been accepted in the United States, along with a renunciation of various other essentials of the democratic process. For all the superiority of the United States in number of atom bombs, our absolute losses are greater because, thanks to the surviving premises of free enterprise, our dispersal has been less effective. American forces in Germany are surrounded and exterminated, despite their offer to surrender or their threats of ultimate retaliation if their surrender is not accepted: their threat is empty because their side has already done its worst. Both countries, in the first shock, suffer severely; but relatively, Russia's losses are less serious than those of the United States; for most of the conditions established under the first hypothesis would still obtain. England, the most vulnerable of the big powers, is not in the path of the great raids, which sweep across the Arctic; but, unmoved by the British proclamation of neutrality, Russia, as an act of precaution, makes a saturation attack on England's chief centers, followed by a series of contamination raids, the purpose of which is to cut the United States off from its main ally and its principal base for organizing a ground operation against Europe.

In both countries, the military establishment, because of its reasonable degree of dispersal, is more intact than the civilian population; but despite the piling up of stores and weapons in the prewar period, the United States forces, precisely because of the technical refinements of their weapons, suffer more quickly than the more primitive Russian organization from the total disorganization of industrial and social life which follows the destruction of urban centers.

On the edges of the old metropolises, life reverts swiftly to a preindustrial level. With forty million people dead in these centers—a few survivors perhaps remember this was General Groves's original estimate—and with no hospital or medical services capable of taking care of the maimed and wounded, the Army is faced with the burden of relief and reorganization, if its own security is not to be ultimately threatened. "Mercy deaths" add to the total holocaust. But the war is not yet over. From bombproof shelters, deep in the Ural Mountains, Russia launches new supplies of atom bombs. This settles down to a war of attrition, which is also a war of nerves. All forms of international intercourse cease throughout the planet; and unfortunately most of the plants for creating synthetic substitutes for natural

17

products located in distant parts of the world have been destroyed; so there is no way of offsetting this loss. In the "island cultures" which appear in the less threatened parts of the world, there is a deliberate relapse into primeval ways: in some places, machines are attacked and disemboweled, and in others they are allowed to fall into complete neglect: in any event, they are treated as symbols of man's decadence, of his will-to-extinction. Free curiosity, invention, innovation, become taboo; and life resumes the repetitious round of tribal society, weighted down by fears even heavier than those Nature alone once occasioned.

Third Assumption: Atomic war does not break out until a sufficient time has elapsed to bring about the atomic armament of the greater part of the civilized world. Not two countries, but at least twenty, are involved in the atomic armament race: Africa, Asia, South America all contribute their quota of suspicion, fear, and death.

On this hypothesis, certain other events may reasonably be predicted: namely, a vast increase in the production of atomic energy, possibly a decrease in the size and weight of the apparatus itself, and even, thanks to the extraordinary concentration on physical research, the utilization of commoner elements hitherto impervious to atomic disintegration. But to keep the prospective horrors within the bounds of the commonplace, I shall not posit the release of atomic energy among the lighter elements. Because of the secrecy that everywhere surrounds atomic experiment, there is much guesswork about the work of rival powers and little diffusion of scientific knowledge: indeed, to guard against diffusion by code and cryptogram or any other kind of indirect exposure, all scientific publication is classified as top secret; and even puzzle magazines and comic magazines are not allowed to leave the country in which they are issued—a precaution that followed a terrible leak through what seemed an entirely innocent channel. Though all this tends to retard atomic investigation, a national concentration of scientific resources on atomic physics and its adjacent spheres in mathematics and chemistry has partly counteracted this tendency.

In every other department of life, there is a slowing down of creativity: worse than that, an active regression. Life is now reduced to purely existentialist terms: existence toward death. The classic otherworldly religions undergo a revival; but even more, quack religions and astrology, with pretensions to scientific certainty, flourish: the tension and anxiety cause even atomic scientists to take refuge in one or another of the new cults. The young who grow up in this world are completely demoralized: they characterize themselves as the generation that drew a blank. The belief in continuity, the sense of a future that holds promises, disappears: certainty of sudden obliteration cuts across every long-term plan, and every activity is more or less reduced to the time span of a single day, on the assumption that it may be the last day. To counteract this, a cult of the archaic and the antiquarian becomes popular: the Victorian period is revived as mankind's Golden Age. Suicides become more frequent, especially among those carrying the weight of responsibility in science and military affairs; and the taking of drugs to produce either exhilaration or sleep becomes practically universal.

In this situation, secrecy gives rise to suspicion and suspicion to uncontrolled fantasies of deception and aggression. Despite the most rigorous immigration barriers, despite the almost complete cessation of foreign travel, rumors that the Communist party has access to the secrets held by other countries, put even the most remote minor officials under the constant surveillance of the FBI; only to encourage the further suspicion, as the ranks of the FBI swell to the dimensions of a considerable army, that Communist influence has also penetrated the FBI. No man trusts his neighbor or dares speak to him freely. Research that turns out to be sterile is regarded as a possible manifestation of treason: those involved in it are purged. Mistakes, failures to achieve production schedules, slips of the tongue, all lead to further purges: the new police state can take no chances. Internationally, an apparent stalemate is reached, because the perfection of an indiscriminate weapon of attack has been followed by the policy of an indiscriminate retaliation on all suspected enemies.

In the threatened atomic war, as in a riot, people will claw and club their neighbors because they have no means of identifying the real culprit and no means of isolating their reaction to him. At first, that universal danger is a restraining influence; but as tension mounts, this becomes the medium for a psychotic outbreak. We will suppose that an atomic explosion takes place either by accident or by deliberate intention; both are definitely possible, and in the very nature of the case, the facts themselves can never be determined. Perhaps a single unbalanced person is responsible for what happens; perhaps a group on the top levels, secret admirers of Hitler, neo-Hitlerians in fact, have decided that the moment has come to establish national supremacy, even if half the world, and half the nation itself, is therewith exterminated. This lights the fuel for a widespread holocaust, one even greater than that originally feared, for meanwhile one or more countries involved has found a way of retarding atomic explosions so that they come not in a moment but in waves of increasing duration:

the blast effect is small but the gamma rays are far more effective. Before the world's atomic stockpiles are exhausted more than half the population of the planet has been killed; and by reason of this high order of radioactive saturation, changes take place in the weather and in the balance of vegetable, animal, insect, and bacterial life; so that the food supply is not sufficient for the random hordes that remain. Death by starvation, or by the drinking of radioactive waters even at points distant from the contaminated areas, slowly destroys more than three-quarters of those who remain.

Now, for the first time in history, the disintegration of civilization takes place on a world-wide scale: no "island cultures" are left to carry on the old processes, even at a reduced level. Within a generation, mankind will enter an age so dark that every other dark age will seem, by contrast, one of intense illumination. Even the animal survival of the species may for long hang in balance. The trauma left on the human psyche will be far worse than that from any previous fear or terror, even the melting of the icecaps. Surviving man will repress his higher functions, not merely his curiosities and his mechanical skills, but his powers of abstraction and symbolism, as threats to his life: he will revert to a stage just this side of the idiot level, a creature of low cunning, focused on the immediate and the concrete, seeking safety in repetition and order, in respect for taboo, ruthlessly killing every variant from this norm, partly losing the use of language itself in his desire to control fresh departures—this will be all that remains of *homo sapiens.* He will survive as an animal with the merest remnant of his intelligence, by eliminating every other capacity that identified him as human.

On this Third Assumption, the damage to the environment might be so complete that man would not have even these diminished alternatives. For if the lower orders of life remained, variations in bacterial enemies, to say nothing of transformations in the human genes, might result in the production of diseases and deformities which would wipe out the surviving members of our species. If that happened, there would be no further social deductions to draw.

Fourth Assumption: Atomic war does not break out at all. But meanwhile, for at least a century, in every part of the earth it remains a growing threat; and the response to this threat is made only in those departments that can be controlled by individual non-cooperative states. The adaptation is complete.

On this hypothesis, the manufacture of atomic weapons has not resulted in violence, destruction, or wholesale extermination; indeed, the very universality of the terror, which almost guaranteed non-resort to war under the Third Assumption, has resulted in something that could be called, in a purely formal sense, peace, and this indefinite suspension of hostilities seems likely to last as long as the total danger that now confronts mankind. Is this, then, the Atomic Golden Age? Let us look at it more closely before we follow General R. W. Johnson's advice to "Dig, son, dig."

It would be needlessly repetitive to describe results already touched on in the Third Assumption; but in the course of a century certain trends, already visible under those conditions, are carried to their logical conclusions. As the danger presses, the plea of the insurance companies and businessmen to hold population in the old centers is first met in the United States by the building of extensive underground shelters and new subway systems. But in New York City, because of its rocky terrain, this process proves too costly to carry through, and that city is the first to be abandoned: its Atomic Age population dwindles to something less than 100,000. At first the Federal government assumes the entire municipal debt and grants a subvention to private owners on a basis of half their assessed values; but this proves too heavy a load, and in engineering the compulsory exodus from the big cities an elaborate pension system is worked out to compensate the still dissatisfied property holders. The nationalization of banks and insurance com-

24

panies is only the first of many more desperate measures to distribute losses. Taxes continue to rise to a point that nullifies financial success; and as soon as the top salaries in the bureaucracy become greater than the maximum net income from private ownership and management, all the earlier advocates of free enterprise become eager for state ownership and flock into the government, where power and privilege are now concentrated.

Presently, the development of the atomic earthquake bomb, capable of penetrating thirty feet of solid concrete and exploding within the earth, makes it plain that any sort of concentration, even underground, is a military liability. Hence the sporadic dispersal of population, which has been taking place, first of all, with military equipment and personnel, gives way to a large-scale effort, using every resource of government, to decentralize and deconcentrate. Under this dispensation, the advocates of the Linear City come into their own. I will not make the picture too grim: let us assume that people continue, where possible, to live and sleep in houses above ground; but all who can afford the luxury, have provided against "the day" by purchasing from the government the standard underground shelter, like the week-end cottage of an earlier day; and the rest of the population has bunks assigned in the underground dormitories. Meanwhile, factories, administrative buildings, schools, in fact almost all collective structures are distributed underground, forming underground road-towns, connected by a transcontinental subway system. Though the invention of the atomic filter provides security against atmospheric contamination, the cost is so prohibitive that, for many years, only the military installations underground are so equipped, even though without such filters all these underground precautions are—against any persistent and thorough saturation—as futile as they are disruptive.

As one of the first precautions against atomic assault, all air traffic of any sort within the country has ceased, except in a few desert areas reserved for military aviation. When a choice has to be made between giving up the airplane or giving up the radar watch that is now maintained day and night along the borders of the entire continent, the atomic danger leaves no question as to which must be abandoned. While in most parts of the country the problem of securing a water supply is readily solved by tapping only underground sources, the likelihood that radioactive materials would be used by an enemy to destroy surface crops and cattle makes it necessary to build up great hydroponic underground farms. Unfortunately the costs are far greater than those of surface farming: another item that demands huge subsidies and in turn still higher taxes. With falling productivity in almost every part of the industrial mechanism, not connected with atomic production or security, the individual standard of living falls, too; and there is a growing tendency among people to desert their posts in the underground collective life in order to scratch for a bare, self-centered, insecure but adventurous living on the surface—although this automatically cuts off the "new pioneers" as they call themselves from every form of social security and pension, and from protection in case atomic war breaks out. When this movement shows signs of becoming a mass reversion to irresponsible primitive life, the government rounds up and shoots every deserter.

Meanwhile, the Constitution of every country is altered, where necessary, so as to give complete control to the military caste. Included in this caste, also in uniform, also sworn to perpetual secrecy, are the scientists and technicians responsible for atomic production and antiatomic defense. Even on the highest levels, the means of creating secrecy—the fragmentation of information and knowledge—prevails. The Chief of Staff, who is ex officio dictator—though in the United States still called, by courtesy, President—appoints his own successor; for he alone is the point at which the jigsaw puzzle of guarded knowledge can be put together. The military

27

caste not only takes over the function of government: it likewise exercises rigorous control over every department of education: at no point can individual initiative or individual opinion be tolerated. By the age of twelve, youths who score high in their aptitude tests are set aside for further training in technological and scientific research along increasingly narrow lines laid down by atomic warfare and its accessory arts. No evasion is possible. Other lines of research are progressively neglected, and, for lack of contact and cross-fertilization of ideas, the quality of research in the physical sciences themselves falls off.

By skillful conditioning, ensured by the centralized control of publication and expression in every form, backed up by constant espionage on conversation, this state of affairs is characterized as freedom, just as the military dictatorship is promoted as the ultimate expression of democracy: one for all and all for one. To make this pill palatable, certain benefits and perquisites are first bestowed on the mass of workers, who at this stage still have organizations capable of striking; but these privileges are soon canceled out by the actual depletion of real wages and decent living standards, and when the workers realize this, they no longer have the means of uniting or even communicating, to register their grievances. Long before this dictatorship is perfected, travel and intercourse between countries has practically disappeared: the police state has become the prison state, and even the jailers do not know what the weather is like on the other side of the prison wall, though many ingenious efforts are made to plant secret agents in other countries.

Because of the all-enveloping quality of the danger, every thought, every action, every plan becomes subservient to the requirements for atomic warfare. Will this fear of a total catastrophe lead to the traditional indifference of the peasants who cultivate their crops on the slopes of Vesuvius? The answer is No, for the peasant's life is free from fear precisely because he continues to do what he always has done, whereas every precaution taken to avert atomic disaster shuts the door to some cherished aspect of normal living and concentrates even the most remote parts of the personality on one theme alone: Fear. The steady increase in atomic destructiveness reaches a point at which everyone realizes that enough potential energy has been stored to destroy all the living spaces of the planet: so as time goes on, the fear becomes more absolute, and—with increased isolation—the prospect of finding a way out becomes more blank.

These conditions—as unfamiliar to the experience of the race as the atom bomb itself—must lead to grave psychological disruptions. We can posit the familiar forms of these regressive reactions: escape in fantasy would be one: purposeless sexual promiscuity would be another: narcotic indulgence would be a third; but perhaps the most disturbing result of this cutting off of the personality from the normal sources and outlets of development would be the frequent outbreaks of catatonic trance; complete resistance to the demands of outward life. Like Bartleby in Melville's story, such people would in effect say, "I know where I am," and have nothing further to do with life. But if the libido were turned outward instead of inward, paranoiac manifestations would probably be universal: suspicion, hatred, aggression, non-cooperation would break out at every level, followed by rounds of murderous violence. In short, the disorders of personality exhibited by the Nazi elite would not merely become universal: they would, if possible, be magnified, though the worst sadism might sometimes be disguised, as with the Nazis, as responsible scientific experimentation with live subjects.

As tension continues to mount, millions of people working below ground begin to show other signs of profound psychological maladjustment for which the current psychological conditioners attached to the General Staff have no adequate answer. Rumors of something more lethal than the atom bomb, impervious to every known means of defense, begin to spread through the catacombs and warrens of this civilization. An epidemic of influenza of a new virulent type creates a fresh wave of terror, because it is suspected to be the work of an unseen and unidentifiable enemy. Hitler's real secret weapon, people say, is at last perfected. A "Let's Die Above Ground" movement begins to spread. Something like a collective attack of claustrophobia breaks out in more than one country almost simultaneously: workers drop their tools and roam around the surface in predatory bands. The very troops who are brought to the surface to combat this subversive movement in more than one case become the victims. Still, no country as yet dares make a wholesale atomic attack. Peace reigns: the rigid peace of death.

On the Fourth Assumption, not a single life has been lost in atomic warfare; nevertheless death has spread everywhere in the cold violence of anticipation, and civilization has been almost as fatally destroyed as it would be under the Third Assumption.

For what is civilization? Civilization is the process whereby a part of mankind threw off the limitations of a rigid, static, tribal society, increased the range of human co-operation, communication, and communion, and created a common instrument for the continued development of the personality and the community. The basis of civilization lies in the fact that energies that were once devoted almost exclusively to physical survival eventually reached a point at which an increasing part of them could be devoted to man's higher functions: instead of submitting to brute necessity, he dominated his environment, he freely remolded his own patterns of living, he created goods and values, purposes and meanings, in short, a common social heritage that other men could share over ever wider reaches of space and time. Men first achieved survival in isolated and restricted groups. Civilization is the never-ending process of creating one world and one humanity.

When secrecy, isolation, withdrawal, and preoccupation with mere physical survival dominate in a society, civilization begins to disintegrate: in the end, the capacity to become human is arrested, if it does not actually disappear, because the very meaning of human life lies in the fulfillment of values and purposes that issue out of past continuities and are directed toward an ever-developing future. Otherwise, the social order becomes a prison and existence therein is punishment for life. That is why the Fourth Assumption turns out, in some ways, to be the most horrible of all: nothing less than a living death. If man fails to take the path toward world co-operation, on every level from government upward, there is no alternative that will not prove monstrous, until the knowledge and intelligence that created our new weapons of extermination are, by one means or another, wiped out. The very precautions men may take for safeguarding life against atomic warfare may also do away with every sound reason for living.

Each of these Assumptions reduces to absurdity the thesis that there is any form of security for individual governments and peoples that can be purchased by their isolated efforts alone, no matter how ready they may be to alter every habit and interest and drive and custom. That way lies suicide. Unconditional co-operation on a world scale is, therefore, the only alternative to the certain disintegration of civilization and the probable extermination of the race.

III

TECHNICS AND THE FUTURE OF
WESTERN CIVILIZATION

If this paper had been given a hundred years ago, its title, even in that fateful year of revolutionary turmoil, 1848, would have been entirely reassuring and its contents hopeful—unless perhaps the topic had been assigned to John Ruskin, for even in that period he perceived that there was thunder on the horizon, as well as dawn. Most educated people a century ago believed that technics, as it came forth in a flood of new inventions, was almost synonymous with Western Civilization; and whether it was or not, there was a positive relation between technical progress and the advance of the human spirit.

Much of that confidence was still present in my youth: altogether naïve yet somehow lovable, like a child's absorption in a plaything he may nevertheless, a day or two later, willfully destroy. That feeling is symbolized for me by one of the lectures my old chemistry professor, Charles Baskerville, used to give on sulphuric acid.

In this lecture, with only the slightest reserve of irony, he advanced the suggestion that the production and consumption of sulphuric acid could be taken as an index of civilization; and he then staged a three-cornered statistical race between Great Britain, Germany, and the United States, which began around the middle of the nineteenth century with Great Britain in the lead and finished—and at this point the class would always break into a spontaneous cheer—with the victory of the United States. In 1914 at the outbreak of World War I the human comfort of that demonstration outweighed its logical defects.

Perhaps it is too early to say that this attitude toward technics has been completely chastened. But at all events it has become plain during the present generation that dissident voices are rising, and those voices are no longer confined to the belated camp followers of Rousseau. Today it is precisely in the departments where our scientific advances have been most decisive, where our technics have been most exquisitely refined—particularly, of course, in nuclear physics—that some of the most eminent exponents of science have begun to sound a note of deep anxiety, as they contemplate the social consequences of technical progress.

The possibility that technics might be misapplied did not apparently bother our Victorian forebears. But no reasonably detached mind can view what has happened all over the world, from Liverpool to Tokyo, the dozens of cities that have been gutted, the millions of human beings who have been coldly exterminated, without questioning the simple faith that scientific knowledge applied to invention would, in Bacon's words, tend to the relief of man's estate. The first of the barbarian invasions has taken place under our eyes; and it differs from those that overcame Rome because the barbarians have sprung up wholly, not partly, from within the society that is attacked. Is it possible, we begin to ask ourselves, that our comic strip hero, Superman, has neither the intelligence nor the moral sensibility to be entrusted with the instruments science has now put at his disposal? Disturbingly enough, the age that produced atomic energy also produced the polluted mind of a Hitler, who was capable, even without the atomic bomb, of conceiving the torture and extermination of some six million Jews alone—to say nothing of the deaths and mutilations he inflicted on millions of people of other nationalities.

Part of my effort here will be to inquire whether within the development of technics itself certain conditions have prevailed which have made these miscarriages possible and in fact almost inevitable; and if so, what changes must take place in Western Civilization as

36

a whole that will make the machine once more the servant and benefactor of life. Certainly it would be unseemly, if not unprofitable, on a genial occasion like the present centennial, to overstress the dark side of the picture. To speak at all about technics today, a certain quality of robust animal faith in the future is necessary. If our civilization were on the edge of extinction, that very fact would rob our present speculations of any lasting significance. Yet as between those who express unlimited confidence in mankind's ability to survive any conceivable series of blunders—a group that contains such wise, competent scholars as A. L. Kroeber, the dean of American anthropologists—and those who believe that without a concerted effort to recover our human balance, our civilization is, in all probability, doomed, as between these two schools I belong—let me confess—to the second group. But that fact does not commit me to more than the wary glance downward a mountain climber may give before he attempts to extricate himself from a tight position by continuing his upward climb. For it remains to those of us who believe that the danger is serious to concentrate, not on potential catastrophes, but on those timely judgments and actions which may keep us from releasing any more of them.

So I purpose to deal mainly in this paper with a group of related special problems that have been raised by the very progress and proliferation of our mechanical and scientific technology during the past century. These problems, I believe, would be serious, indeed in some ways overwhelming, even if they had not been magnified by thirty years of warfare, barbarism, and extermination; and even if we were not now possibly on the brink of racial suicide, thanks to the fact that through the knowledge of biotic and atomic energies we now command, we in the United States alone, to look no further afield, hold powers of life and death over mankind: separated from their use by only the thinnest walls of habit, taboo, intelligence, and moral enlightenment. Yet if we recognize the existence of these essential problems promptly, and if by some further stroke of intelligence we give heed to them, that fact will go a long way toward lifting the dangers which our overt instruments of mass extermination have conjured up.

Without further ado, I purpose to treat these underlying problems under three main heads: first, the problem of time, space, and power; second, deriving from this, the general problem of quantity and quantification; and finally, the problem of automatism. The solution of these internal problems of technics seems to me essential for the integration of our mechanical functions into a new over-all social design, based on a different set of human motives and purposes than those which played so large a part in creating the age of the machine. All these problems form a budget of very teasing paradoxes; and not the least paradox, I fear, will be my final conclusion, that only by a deliberate act of restrictive self-discipline on the part of science and technics, will the human agents concerned be able to concentrate sufficiently on those decisive inventions in the realm of morals, politics, and psychological direction which will restore the balance to our civilization as a whole. *To save technics itself we shall have to place limits on its heretofore unqualified expansion.* But I must not anticipate.

Probably the most decisive change modern technics has brought about, certainly the most pervasive, is the change it has effected in both our concepts and our experience of space, time, energy. Most of the inventions that Leonardo and Bacon and della Porta and Glanvill correctly anticipated, and a grand succession of later inventors realized, were devices for saving time, for shrinking space, for enhancing energy, for speeding motions, for accelerating natural processes: devices which equipped modern man with seven-league boots and magic carpets, releasing people from the physical constraints of here and now. But note the curious twist that actual experience has given to all these early plans and aspirations: the faster we travel, the less we actually see and experience on the way; the larger the area of our communication, other things remaining the same, the more limited the area of understanding; the greater our physical power, the more formidable become our social and moral limitations.

As soon as we achieve the theoretic goal of annihilating distance entirely—as we now do for all practical purposes even without television when we telephone overseas—we come back again precisely to where we started: to the village world of face-to-face contact with over two billion villagers for neighbors, and at that point our human weaknesses, serious enough in a village society, become magnified far more rapidly than our virtues, by reason of the technical process itself; just as a public-address system, blaring to the world from a family dinner table, would accentuate its trivialities and bickerings rather than the less visible processes of love and devotion. Thanks to technics, men have become physically neighbors to people on the other side of the earth; but we have done little to make ourselves mental neighbors or to train ourselves in habits of courtesy, in disciplines of mutual forbearance, which would keep us in amicable relations.

In their too unwary innocence, the founders of modern technics did not anticipate these difficulties; or doubtless they would have done something to head them off. When the Royal Society was founded in England, you will recollect, its members deliberately decided to reject any collaboration with those disciplines which would now be called the social sciences and the humanities. For their purposes, it was possible to leave out of account every human impulse and need, except those which were actively engaged in either the exploration or the exploitation of the physical environment. That decision, symbolic of a thousand others that accompanied the stunningly triumphant but one-sided advance of technics, has had the result of limiting the benefits we might legitimately expect from our present mastery of time and space. From Francis Bacon onward, people thought that the advance of technics would by itself automatically solve the crucial problems of civilization: with unlimited production, they thought, we could by-pass the moral problem of just distribution, with unlimited physical means of travel, we would by the mere multiplication of contacts make men brothers.

Certainly, the whole development of man himself, from small tribal units to cities and nations, from nations to leagues, unions, and empires, has been in the direction of unity and universality, and throughout history this development has been handicapped, up to modern times, by a technics so unprogressive that it had reached its premedieval plateau very largely before the Bronze Age. But precisely at the point where tech-nics, thanks to Henry and Faraday and Morse and Watt, had caught up with the universal vision of the great religious teachers, our social facilities, so far from keep-ing pace with technical invention, actually went back-ward.

The very language, Latin, which had enabled Euro-pean scholars to communicate freely beyond their na-tional boundaries, was allowed to lapse before we had invented a simpler and more universal vehicle of com-munication. Here we face another bitter paradox. For what is the use of being able to speak to another person instantaneously on the other side of the planet if we have no common language and if we have no common purpose, except that of exterminating our distant brother before he seizes the initiative and exterminates us? We have left the problem of creating a universal language mainly to a few amateurs and fanatics who naturally have so far made little headway, although with our present skills in comparative philology and logical analysis, the problem of inventing such a language pre-sents far fewer difficulties than did the original invention of the alphabet.*

* *Interlingua*, a somewhat more polyglot version of Peano's *Latino Sine Flexione*, is an excellent halfway house, vastly superior to Esperanto: but it is not based on principles that would ensure its stable use as a universal language.

The point I am making here touches almost every field of technical advance. None of our marvelous technical instruments and processes can function efficiently except in a society that has provided adequate social destinations and outlets. When technical advances are not co-ordinated with social advances, the result of an overconcentration on technics may be social confusion, frustration, retrogression. The contradiction of the motorcar, capable of going seventy-five miles an hour, reduced to the ignominious crawl of a pedestrian on the crowded avenues of our cities, can be matched in almost every other department. If this fact has been slow in coming home to us, the sudden increase in the potentialities for mass destruction and mass extermination, through the invention of the atom bomb, has driven the point in; for to turn such an instrument loose on society, without erecting fresh moral safeguards and controls, in particular without creating an effective system of world government, was an act of incredible social irresponsibility; although it only brought to a climax a whole train of such acts since the beginning of the paleotechnic revolution.

Now it is precisely in the most advanced parts of our technics that the mischief of treating technical development as an end in itself becomes most plain. For neither radio nor supersonic planes make sense until we realize that all men are brothers, and that every nation and group, however isolated in appearance, is part of an infinitely complicated and involved ecological partnership of planetary dimensions. In the sixth century B.C. the group of world religions that took form were for long theoretically far in advance of technology in their universalism and in their sense of a common moral law binding mankind together. Unfortunately, the persistent cultural lag between the machine and our religious and moral concepts is now visible in quite another manner than Professor William Fielding Ogburn believed, when he first used this term: for our technics has become universal in an ideological epoch that has turned to the worship of the false tribal gods of nationalism. We discarded the universal insights of Confucius and Buddha, of Mo Ti and St. Paul, at the very moment they were most needed to make technics a true agent of civilization.

Certainly, if there is any department where the fact of human interdependence should be recognized, fully and generously, it is in technics itself. For the whole fabric of modern technology rests on a foundation of world-wide collaboration: with the result that multiple discoveries and inventions, in widely separated countries, are commonplaces of our technical development. Yet in this very field nationalism of the most abysmally tribal kind has muffled the plain facts. We Western

44

peoples, to begin with, have talked as if modern technics were wholly the work of our own culture, indeed, of the last few centuries of our culture; whereas the scientific basis of our technology goes back directly to the Arabs and the Hindus and the Greeks; our most decisive inventions, like the printing press and the internal combustion engine, come from the Orient; while without the extra lift to the food supply, given by the Amerindian culture, through the potato and maize, we might have lacked part of the physical vitality necessary to produce our modern achievements. If one removed from modern technics a single raw material, rubber, originally the product of a backward tribe of Amazonian Indians who had themselves produced rubber raincoats and syringes, our whole economy would almost come to a halt. In other words, modern technics is a product of a world-wide collaboration; and unless we extend such collaboration and make it firmer, our civilization will within a measurable time go downhill.

Even within Western Civilization itself people often talk as if some single nation had a monopoly on invention: this solecism reaches a peak of error in the very common notion that the atom bomb is an exclusively American contrivance, instead of what it actually is, the product of our whole scientific culture, contemporary and historic, and even in its final stages more immediately in debt to a German, Meitner, a Dane, Bohr, a Hungarian, Szilard, and an Italian, Fermi, than to our own workers in the same field. Patent offices create national monopolies, and immigration laws and tariff acts often erect barriers against the free movement of men and goods; but an advanced technics, such as we have created during the last century, depends upon a world-wide circulation of ideas; and unless that world-wide basis is maintained, the collecting reservoirs will be so lowered that only a trickle of inventions will come forth.

Now I turn more specifically to the problem of quantity. Though this problem derives largely from our expansion of power and our mechanical conquest of space and time, it invades every department of technics where the methods of mass production have been successfully installed. In general, the advance of the machine has been accompanied by a general quantification of life. One of the reasons for this issues forth directly from the assumptions upon which our whole mechanical world picture was based: for science, following Galileo, turned its back on the so-called secondary qualities, as ephemeral, subjective, and in any scientific sense, meaningless —unless, like color, they could be translated into measurable units. From this point of view norms, patterns, ideals, were wholly unimportant: the only intelligent questions one could ask about the physical world were those relating to quantity, and the only acceptable answers those ascertainable by measurement. Hence the capitalist's interest in quantity—his belief that there are no natural limits to acquisition—was supplemented, in technology, by the notion that quantitative production had no natural limits either: norms, limits, optimum amounts, goals, were out of the picture.

Considering the precarious conditions under which the greater portion of the human race had previously lived, the miserable dearth and scarcity and near-starvation, the besetting anxiety of trying to make both ends meet, one can well understand this new preoccupation with quantity. Just as the unlimited land of the New World promised food to the hungry, so the apparently unlimited productivity of the machine promised to make all men as wealthy, and therefore presumably as happy, as kings. Here once more our lack of concern for the social destination of the machine has curbed its real promises, as John Stuart Mill mordantly observed even at the height of Victorian optimism. For this society, which had learned the mechanical art of multiplication, had neglected the ethical art of division: hence, though the condition of the worker actually improved, it did not do so sufficiently to counteract his discontents or overcome his natural anxieties.

But that familiar problem I bring up here only to lay

it aside for one that has as yet gained far less recognition: the effect of uncontrolled quantitative production when the system of distribution *is* fully adequate. This is, perhaps, an even more difficult problem to solve; indeed impossible without ethical criteria and human restraints, and to bring it home I shall draw my concrete example from one of the oldest departments of mass production and standardization: that of printing. No single invention, probably, has had more radical effects upon the social order than printing from movable types; for at one stroke it broke the class monopoly of culture for the first time: he who learned to read progressively had access to every part of the social heritage in a society whose boundaries were in process of continued extension. That was, without doubt, a gigantic social gain; for it laid the basis not merely for a democratic system of government but for a democratic culture; just as the machine generally, by raising the burden of servile human labor, had made it possible to achieve leisure and education without slavery.

Nevertheless, this great invention has brought penalties that have, only in our own time, become fully apparent. I do not refer to the dangers of surplus production, to the gluts and overflows of the market: I refer to the fact that even under the best economic arrangements, we still have evolved no rational means for controlling, either at source or at destination, the current output of printed matter and reducing it to humanly manageable dimensions. Before the printing press was invented, the difficulty of reproducing manuscripts by hand automatically reduced the quantity of books in circulation: often probably to a much lower point than was intellectually or socially desirable. But by now just the opposite of this has happened: the mere multiplication of our mechanical facilities has so swollen the output of printed matter, that if any human being attempted to keep up with it in the most cursory way he would have no time left for any other activity.

The result is another paradox, sometimes called, as William Cobbett first called it, "starvation in the midst of plenty": one might also characterize it as the poverty of overproductivity. So far we have invented only two minor devices for lessening some of the minor defects of this plenitude: one is the useful but nevertheless dangerous habit of skimming; the other is the device of specialization. Each specialist, by agreement, pays attention to the narrow column of water that works his particular turbine, and automatically rejects contributions that flow in any other channels: even as he turns aside, perhaps more decisively, from the broad silt-laden river of human experience from which all these activities derive. This last situation is far from satisfactory, first because it assumes that interrelationships are unimportant and that an over-all view is unnecessary; and second, because in any single department of thought, no matter how specialized, the same paralyzing over-productivity is manifest. Either to explore the past or keep up with the present becomes increasingly impossible: so that our capacity for assimilation may be said to vary inversely with our capacity for production; and eventually this will have an unfortunate effect upon our creativity, indeed on our very rationality. When our frustrations finally become acute, we may be tempted, like Hitler's followers, to seek in mere charlatanism and quackery some short cut to order.

Let no one imagine that there is a mechanical cure for this mechanical disease. Only politeness would keep me from characterizing this desperate hope as wishful thinking; for the fact is that the attempt to cope with quantification by publishing compendiums, abstracts, synopses, from *Science Abstracts* to the *Reader's Digest* or their hundred imitations, or the alternative device of using microfilm, instead of books, are all but sorry stopgaps: indeed, they themselves merely become a further problem. The introduction of these ingenious mechanical facilities has about the same effect that results from the widening of a crowded traffic artery in a city: it actually increases the amount of traffic the avenue will have to bear and in the long run aggravates the very condition it set out to cure. No: the fact is that here, as in so many other departments, there is no purely mechanical solution for the problem of quantification: the answer must in fact be framed in qualitative terms, not by inventing a new machine, but by transforming the purposes and values of the human agent who uses it.

Why should we gratuitously assume, as we so constantly do, that the mere existence of a mechanism for manifolding or mass production carries with it an obligation to use it to the fullest capacity? If we are not to court mental obfuscation, indeed complete paralysis, we must learn to exercise, first of all, a certain continence and discipline in publication, printing nothing by way of routine, nothing because we have a schedule to meet and pages to fill, nothing merely for the doubtful luster and glory of getting our names into print a sufficient number of times each year to jog the attention of our peers and our administrative superiors. To achieve control, we shall even, I suspect, have to reconsider and perhaps abandon the whole notion of periodical publication, particularly by week or month, as a possibly needless incitement to premature or superfluous publication. I do not intend to canvass all the professional and personal devices that we might invent to meet this situation. What I do insist upon is that we cannot continue inertly to accept a burdensome technique of overproduction without inventing a social discipline for handling it; and that until we do this our situation will steadily worsen.

What applies so plainly to mass printing applies in equal or even greater degree to almost every other department of mass production. Our production levels in every field must be based, not on the physical capacities of our machines to multiply goods, but on the psychological capacities of the human organism to assimilate them and convert them ultimately into an orderly, purposive, rational, and significant life. Without such a hierarchy of life needs and values, without the constant subordination of technics to human purpose, the present tempo of mechanical production can result only in an increasing misdirection and nullification of power and effort.

The control of quantity is bound up with still another problem, likewise derived from our very success. Every technical process tends, in its perfection, to eliminate the active worker from participation and to produce an effective substitute: the automaton. The original model for all our automatic machines is the mechanical clock; and machinery approaches perfection as it takes on the regularity, the self-regulation, the uniformity in production, that a good chronometer achieves. But the notion of a self-regulating mechanism, performing its own functions, not subject to direct human intervention or control, has spread from simple machines to the whole process. The tendency in mass production is to transfer initiative and significance from the worker who once operated the machine to the machine that operates the worker. As the process becomes more highly rationalized, on its own narrow terms, the worker becomes, as it were, de-rationalized; and this applies on every level of organization.

By now we have discovered that there are serious drawbacks in this process, which were not evident in its earlier stages: not the least is that increasingly the only way in which men can assert their specifically human qualities, once they are engaged by an automatic process, is by nonparticipation, by resistance, by throwing a monkey wrench into the works. This limiting of the power of rational participation, and therefore rational control, tends likewise to produce a sense of impotence: once a process is in motion, once a product is, so to say, in the works, everyone feels that nothing can be done to alter the end product or to halt the operation. While people have little doubt that human intention, human will, start the process of invention and production, they have become so deeply the victim of their own automatism that they tend blindly to deny that human intention

53

and human effort may also bring the process to an end or change its direction, once it has been fixed. That fact is as dangerous in the present crisis as the ideological conflicts that are at work.

Do not, I beg you, misunderstand the bearings of this argument. For me, as for the most ardent apologist for the machine, the automaton is Western Civilization's decisive answer to the problem Aristotle propounded— on what terms can human slavery be brought to an end? Furthermore, our knowledge of the wisdom of the body, as Dr. Walter Cannon called it, leaves no doubt as to the benefits of automatic processes in any kind of vital economy: automatic machines and organizations are as useful to society as the system of nervous reflexes and endocrines is to the human body: both forms of automatism leave the mind free for the exercise of its higher functions. But in individual men, the condition for successful automatism is fulfilled by an over-all agency, the brain, which may intervene when necessary and resume the functions of government: evaluation and conscious direction.

Unfortunately, the tendency of automatism is to make the human purposes subordinate to the very means originally erected to serve them. Let me give you a very trivial example of this perversion: I wish I could also say that it is an uncommon one. A friend of mine went to a hospital for observation, to determine the cause of certain disturbing physical symptoms: after making a series of exhaustive tests, spinal fluid examination, blood counts, sedimentation tests, and so forth, the physicians by a chemical analysis of the blood finally hit upon the source of her strange ailment, which turned out to be simple carbon monoxide poisoning, due to a defective furnace flue in her home. Meanwhile the untainted air of the hospital had improved her condition and her complete cure could be ensured by calling in the steam fitter to repair the furnace; so she was promptly dismissed. A week later, however, she received an urgent call from the hospital: they wanted her to report without delay for another examination. A little puzzled, my friend explained that there was nothing the matter with her, her ailment had not returned; but the hospital remained insistent. "You must come back here tomorrow," the secretary patiently explained, "to have your Wassermann taken. The nurse forgot to check this, and our records are incomplete."

This tendency to overlook the human end which our automatic organizations serve has begun to pervade our whole civilization; and in the end, if it is uncorrected, it may effectually undermine our best achievements. For the fact is that standardization, organization, automatism, which are the real and special triumphs of modern technics, tend with their very perfection to produce routineers: people whose vital interests and activities lie outside the system to which they have committed themselves. The vice that dogged the regularities and automatisms of monastic life in the Middle Ages, the vice called *acedia,* or lethargic indifference, already tends to creep into the older, staler departments of our technology. For one Robert Young who tries to awaken his colleagues from their somnolent routine, there are ten anti-Youngs in the railroad system and elsewhere, whose secret motto is: "Anything for a quiet life." Unless extraneous jolts and challenges awaken such people, as war awakens an army from its paper-shuffling and button-polishing, their indifference, and their more active boredom, may in time produce an over-all loss of efficiency. Only innocents fancy that the practice of feather-bedding is confined to trade unions.

When we eliminate the active human factor in industry, in other words, we may also eliminate, with all but fatal success, the impulses, passions, drives, and aspirations that make for continued technical perfection. This possibility has been amply demonstrated by the work of many investigators, beginning in a crude way with early efficiency engineers like Gantt, and going forward in such inquiries as those Professor Elton Mayo conducted in the famous Western Electric experiment at

Hawthorne. No matter how marvelous our inventions, how productive our industries, how exquisitely automatic our machines, the whole process may be brought to a standstill by its failure fully to engage the human personality or to serve its needs. During the nineteenth century technics often served as a substitute for religion and love: the machine was to some a god, commanding obedience, to others a mistress, evoking passionate pursuit and affectionate loyalty: in any case a refuge from the vexatious problems of human destiny, of life and death.

But with the exception of states like Soviet Russia, still in the throes of industrial pioneering, full of child-like delight in the mere go of machines, that innocent faith and that attitude no longer prevail. In addition to doing its daily job, technics no longer serves as a religious system of redemption and salvation. At the end of his Faust, the great humanist, Goethe, preached the new doctrine of salvation by works: meaning by works, in so many words, engineering works, like the draining of marshes and the cutting through of canals: indeed, he confessed to Eckermann, toward his end, that he would like to live on another half century so that he might behold the cutting through of the Suez and Panama canals. Does that confession not seem pathetically naïve today? Would a man on the brink of the grave now wish to prolong his life, so that he might see the first full-scale use of the atom bomb? Or the first widespread trial of bacteria in unrestricted genocide? On the contrary, these very possibilities cast a doubt on the whole process to which we have so wholeheartedly committed our civilization. If once our automatism led us to such suicidal conclusions, mankind might recoil from the machine itself, precisely as Samuel Butler predicted under cover of satire in *Erewhon*.

Is there any way of circumventing such a crisis? Is there any alternative to such a dismal backward step? Yes. The answer is to exert a mighty effort, here and now, to correct the internal weaknesses that threaten our society. Part of this answer must come from within the world of technics itself: part from our culture as a whole: in both cases it will demand a shift from mechanical criteria to biological and human criteria. As for the first, many correctives have already appeared in our technology, as a growing interest in living processes has supplemented our original concentration on the physical world. Thanks to the development of biological, sociological, and psychological science, we are often equipped with alternative ways of performing the same task, or reaching the same end: just as a psychiatrist, confronted with a neurotic patient, may in treatment of certain cases have a choice of electrical shock (a mechanical device), of insulin shock (a chemical device), of psychoanalysis (a psychological device), or vocational and sociodramatic therapy (a sociological device). Surgeons once performed elegant operations on the stomach and duodenum that are now more happily treated by a correct diet or even psychological guidance. As soon as we transfer attention, within technics, from the machine to the personality and the community, that shift will itself introduce regulative and normative standards into every operation. But as yet, unfortunately, only a small sector of our technics has escaped the narrowing influence of its original mechanical preoccupations.

Such internal changes in technics, however, will remain secondary to a larger change in our culture as a whole: for no part of our technics is self-sustaining, and no part is unaffected by decisions we make in other departments of our culture—decisions of a moral, esthetic, religious, or political nature. Our situation today calls for a development of the repressed and dwarfed functions of the human personality, on a sufficient scale to restore the ecological balance that technics has disrupted. Unlimited profit and unlimited power can no longer be the determining elements in technics, if our civilization as a whole is to be saved: social and personal development must take precedence. Not the

59

Power Man, not the Profit Man, not the Mechanical Man, but the Whole Man, Man in Person, so to say, must be the central actor in the new drama of civilization. This means that we must reverse the order of development which first produced the machine: we must now explore the world of history, culture, organic life, human development, as we once explored the nonliving world of nature. We must understand the organics and psychics of personality as we first understood the statics and mechanics of physical processes. We must center attention on quality, value, pattern, and purpose, as we once centered attention on quantity, on mechanical order, on mass and motion.

If technics is not to play a wholly destructive part in the future of Western Civilization we must now ask ourselves, for the first time, what sort of society and what kind of man are we seeking to produce? About any and every machine, above all about the technical process itself, the critical question is: How much does this instrument further life? If it does not promote human welfare, in the fullest sense, an atomic pile is as disreputable as a pinball game or a jukebox. In short: we must do justice to the whole nature of man before we can make the most of our mechanical improvements. The restoration of the organic, the human, the personal, to a central place in our economy, is essential if we are to overcome the forces that, without such over-all direction and control, are now driving our society ever closer to internal disintegration and external destruction.

Our civilization has now reached the point predicted by one of its most acute analysts, Henry Adams, more than a generation ago. Making rough calculations as to the acceleration of social processes through the expansion of energy alone, through successive inventions in water power, steam, electricity, Adams believed that the final change of phase, from the electric phase to one based on inordinate power of cosmic magnitude, would be a brief one: either it would end in the downfall of civilization or the emergence of an entirely different social order.

We have lived to see most of Adams's uncanny predictions fully verified. The only hope for saving a society so threatened from untimely extinction, will be a swift recoil from the ideas and forces and processes that have brought about this dangerous state of unbalance. If such a recoil takes place in time, most of what is humanly valuable in our scientific and technical advance will be saved: just as most of classic civilization might have been saved if, in the first century A.D., the Romans had dedicated themselves to a new way of life, based on the primacy of the person, which Christianity introduced at too late a period to save the body of classic culture. But if we passively submit to the automatic processes that are already in motion, then the end of Western Civilization is already in sight.

The guiding principle of the last century was summed up in the title of a notable book recently published by the Swiss scholar, Dr. Sigfried Giedion: *Mechanization Takes Command*. But if Western Civilization is to overcome the disruptive forces that have issued forth from the very processes in which it has taken most pride, from which it has looked for the relief of man's estate and indeed his personal salvation, we will have to take for our guiding principle in the future a quite different motto: Let Man Take Command. Instead of continuing to mechanize and regiment man, we must undertake just the opposite operation; we must humanize the machine, restoring lifelike attributes, the attributes of selectivity, balance, wholeness, autonomy, and freedom, in every department where work must be done. To follow that course, in all its ramifications and implications, will be to lay down the foundations for a new age: not the ultimate Age of the Machine, as pictured by the cockeyed writers of science fiction, but the first real Age of Man.

IV

"MIRACLE" OR CATASTROPHE

The story of the atom bomb and other scientific forms of genocide has not yet been told. But already it is plain that there is a Sunday-school moral tagged at the end of it. This is the story of a pride that begot blindness and of infinite power that became impotence, for the kind of intelligence that has invented and exploited the bomb has so far shown no aptitude for controlling its undesirable social results. Instead of expediting our preparations for peace, our new weapons have absorbed the thought and energy of our national government in further preparations for war. Unless we understand the moral of this story fully and face all its implications honestly, we shall not be able to correct the succession of military and political blunders we have perpetrated in three short years.*

With the invention of the atom bomb, the United States stepped into a role on the international stage not unlike

* This article was written in 1948. Its criticisms are not the product of hindsight; nor are its proposals a belated attempt to find an answer to Russia's possession of nuclear weapons, though the Communist world's new strength in this field perhaps gives support to the argument.

that of the Emperor Jones in Eugene O'Neill's play. We believed, officially, that the atom bomb made us invulnerable; but as we stumbled through the jungle of the postwar world, secure in this self-imposed delusion, we gradually lost our own sense of direction; presently, as night overtook us, menacing fears and specters arose in our own minds, making ever louder the ominous beat of the distant Russian war drums. None of our wild random shots has caused these frightening images to disappear; and at the end, we find that we have nothing left by way of an effective answer to our fears except the magic of a silver bullet: the atom bomb. Perhaps the figure would be a little more accurate if one said that we have a whole cartridge belt of silver bullets; but like so many of the magic gifts in ancient fairy stories, there is an unexpected penalty attached to their use: the result of using all of them might be to wipe out our friends and allies as well as our enemy. In O'Neill's play, you will remember, silver bullets killed the Emperor Jones. They were fired by savages who had copied his magic.

After several years of thinking and planning in terms of magic, there are signs that the American Government has at last begun to grasp its limitations. If the President's call for rebuilding our armed forces means anything, it means that his advisers now realize that the atom bomb, so far from being able to curb Soviet Russia's expansion, has stepped up all that country's plans for dominating Europe. Possibly they also realize that we would need an immense army to conquer and police Russia after successfully using the atom bomb: so that the notion of the atom bomb as a labor-saving device, which would do away with the most unpopular aspects of military power—the fact that it demands universal service and the heavy sacrifice of human life—must now be discarded as another delusion of pride.

So far we have talked peace while every action has hastened war. Perhaps if we have the courage to talk war, we may yet face the task we have funked these last three years: creating the foundations of genuine peace. The purpose of this article is to outline a series of operations which could, conceivably, cause the United States and Soviet Russia to compose their differences and work for a common end. To show why these operations cannot be evaded, let us review the entire situation.

The most important fact about World War II is that in the course of fighting it the ancient art of warfare gave way to the increasing practice of genocide. Following the theory and practice of our Fascist enemies, whose moral nihilism destroyed the very principle of restraint, the democratic powers took over genocide or mass extermination.

Now genocide is war's ancient and more bestial rival;

but up to the present decade, it could only be carried out by slow, tedious, handicraft methods. All through history mass extermination had indeed been practiced on a limited scale, even by such a highly civilized people as the Athenians: witness their slaughter of the entire male population of Melos after that island surrendered; but fortunately for mankind, the profits of slavery and the moral restraints of Christianity reduced to the vanishing point the practice of mass extermination. In our time, genocide was brought back on a considerable scale by the Turks, even before the Nazis introduced the methodical horrors of their extermination camps, with their record of six to seven million Jewish victims alone. But it remained for World War II to bring about the general adoption of random and unrestricted extermination.

The hypocrisy of our age, which has sought to make barbarism palatable by applying traditional and honorable names to its practices, as the Russians call their savage despotism "democracy," has led us to call mass extermination by a false name: total war. As was early set forth by the Italian General Douhet, seeking to make the fullest employment of air power, "total war" sought to bring about the results of a military victory, not by engaging the enemy's armies primarily, but by terrorizing and exterminating the civilian population, at the smallest possible risk to the aggressor. When this method was first used by the Fascist powers in their bombing of Madrid, Warsaw, London, Rotterdam, and Coventry, almost every American regarded genocide as the monstrosity it actually is: up to 1942 the American army even boasted of the fact that it practiced only "pinpoint" bombing of selected military targets. But before the war ended, the military forces of the United States had multiplied the technical weapons of mass extermination and had employed them on an even more devastating scale than the Fascists had done—if one leaves out the mass production statistics of the Nazi crematories. A single ordinary bomb raid on Tokyo caused 180,000 casualties in a single night. The atom bomb only wrapped up this method of extermination in a neater, and possibly cheaper, package.

Not the least extraordinary fact about the postwar period is that mass extermination has awakened so little moral protest. It is as if the Secretary of Agriculture had authorized the sale of human meat, during the meat shortage, and everyone had accepted cannibalism in daily practice as a clever dodge for reducing the cost of living. Conceivably a quick moral revulsion against the further employment of genocide would have taken place in America if Soviet Russia had alone invented the atom bomb. Unfortunately, the failure to understand the change in method and purpose that has taken place through the transformation of warfare into genocide has given an air of specious unreality to all our plans for controlling the production of atomic energy. For it is not the atom bomb, but our willingness to use any instruments of genocide that constitutes the all-enveloping danger. Long before the present age, invading armies could have poisoned the civilian water supply of their enemies, if extermination had been their object: they could have used all our own transparent excuses, too: would it not have saved their soldiers' lives and shortened the war? But, in fact, the taboo against poisoning the water supply was seldom violated: indeed, it remained so absolute it survived World War II. Because today all life-preservative taboos have been lifted, radioactive water has become the ideal medium of mass extermination. As for our biological weapons, should a plague break out during the next five years, comparable to that of influenza in 1918, no one would know if it were the result of wholly natural causes, or the preliminary softening up practiced by an aggressive enemy.

The outcome of this development is already visible. If militant genocide does not turn the planet into an extermination camp, its potentialities for breeding fear and suspicion may turn it into a madhouse, in which the physicians in charge will be as psychotic as the patients. Since all preparations for mass extermination must be secret, we readily tend to project upon our enemies our own plans for aggression. On an alarming scale, this transformation has already taken place. Our fear of Russia is proportionate to the damage we believe ourselves capable of inflicting on Russia, and the very secrecy that our own weapons impose only weakens the possibilities of rational control.

The conquest of Germany came about mainly through the use of the classic instruments of warfare: Russia's immense contribution to this victory leaves no doubt of that fact. But the general cessation of fighting left the United States with undisputed pre-eminence in the production of instruments of extermination, including bacterial weapons we had not actually employed: and at that moment a combination of technical curiosity and political irresponsibility caused us to make an erroneous choice. We hastily dismantled our army and navy, and even reduced our air forces. The theory that this was brought about wholly by public clamor to have our boys return home will not bear close inspection; for that need not have disrupted the whole apparatus of selective service. What caused this hasty disintegration was the smug belief that the atom bomb now gave us all the protection we needed. With the atom bomb up our sleeve, our leaders believed that we could "contain"

Russia: here and there in Washington circles there were even voices that proclaimed that a few timely atom bombs dropped on the Kremlin would enable the United States to live happily ever afterward.

If the testimony of the nuclear physicists had been heeded, these illusions would never have flourished. In an extremely able memorandum, submitted to President Roosevelt just before his death in 1945, Dr. Leo Szilard pointed out that as soon as we disclosed our possession of atomic energy by dropping the atom bomb we should start an arms race in atomic weapons which would progressively decrease our own security. That warning, in varied forms, was repeated many times before the Senate Atomic Committee in the winter of 1945-1946 by the scientists who produced the bomb: they pointed out that the use of atomic weapons must constantly increase the insecurity of the United States: some of them added that it would be well to forgo atomic energy itself for as much as ten or fifteen years, in order to have time to devise a foolproof means of international control and co-operation: nearly all made the creation of an effective world government the first step toward achieving real security and durable peace. For them, world government was no longer a "maybe" but a must. In spite of the almost frantic efforts to awaken the country made by the chief atomic scientists, headed by Einstein, their advice remained unheeded. Without adequate discussion, without debate, above all without understanding the final consequences to all our democratic institutions, we delayed taking the necessary steps to force a showdown: a showdown which would make it possible to transform the United Nations into World Government. Instead, while blandly talking peace, we committed ourselves to expanding our own production of instruments of mass extermination. If our armed forces now have so little to show for the billions a year they claimed for their "peacetime" activities, this decision perhaps explains it. Weapons of genocide are not placed on parade.

From 1945 on, the United States, by every conceivable act and gesture, from the premature shutting off of lend-lease to the hasty dismantling of its armies, turned its back to war. By that act, we undermined the foundations of peace. Because of the very fears our own weapons of extermination had planted in ourselves, our international policy was, from beginning to end, riddled with ambiguities, contradictions, and double talk. We talked about peaceful co-operation in the United Nations, but we seized advance bases at the dictation of our navy and announced that our actions could not be profitably discussed: we spoke up boldly on behalf of freedom and democracy, but let Russia come forward as the advocate of colonial peoples and the champion of racial equality: we proclaimed our readiness to share all the secrets of atomic energy production, through the creation of a World Atomic Authority, at the same time that we disclosed we had even more deadly means of mass extermination. While announcing our purpose to combat Communism, we asked Russia to throw her doors open to international inspection of the most continuous and rigid kind; and in the interests of future military campaigns against Russia, we pursued a policy of appeasing Fascism in Spain, South America, and now— worst of all—in Germany, with our abandonment of our decartelization policy and our benign buildup of the Nazis' most dangerous accomplices, the big German industrialists.

Whatever may be said for this policy, it was not the way in which an intelligent nation would proceed if it aimed to produce a united and peaceful world. Meanwhile, in our single-minded campaigns against Soviet Russia, we forgot the needs and interests of our closest friends. Leaving our allies to flounder about in hopeless poverty, exhausted in body and spirit, overworked and underfed, with their industrial plants and transportation systems in ruins, we returned greedily to our fleshpots: bigger fleshpots than ever since, thanks to centralized governmental planning and enormous government investment, our industrial capacity had, in the teeth

of stubborn opposition by our so-called free enterpris-
ers, been doubled in the course of the war. To make our
position even more odious, we attributed the results of
governmental enterprise and military good luck to the
virtues of American capitalism, while we attached to
socialism the odium of low productivity due actually to
the destruction and exhaustion of war—a war whose
worst civilian consequences to ourselves were to reduce
our consumption of coffee and gasoline. These methods
brought their own reward. Instead of containing Russia,
we confused and weakened the democratic opposition to
Russia; and instead of insuring peace we intensified the
military struggle for "position." Up to the announcement of the Marshall Plan, our policy was wholly a
negative one.

The consequences of this bipartisan policy are now
plain: as Mr. Bernard Baruch has pointed out, the
United States and Soviet Russia are really at war: cold
war is to hot war as water is to steam. Unfortunately,
our army equipped itself between 1945 and 1948 to
practice extermination rather than war; and as a result
Russia, by confining herself to the classic means of
warfare, diplomatic, psychological, and military, has
won all the opening rounds. In a series of limited moves,
too small in compass to warrant our immediate use of
the atom bomb by way of reply, Russia has improved

both her political and her military position. While the American army in its recent form must wait for the moment when it might (theoretically) score a knockout, Soviet Russia has been winning steadily on points. Doubtless, even without the dread of a surprise atomic attack, the dynamics of Russian totalitarianism, czarist in origin, would have prompted her further aggression and expansion, if only to preserve her own reactionary political state from fatal competition with the more progressive democracies. But the fact is that we have played into the Russian government's hands by giving them large and pressing incentives for hastening their expansion.

Meanwhile, the very nature of Russia's response has increased even the military hazards of our own situation; and it has fairly effectively neutralized the one type of weapon on which we have dwelt with such obsessive emphasis. For if the keynote to the next war is mass extermination, with no holds barred, then our only secure advance base in Europe, England, is now threatened as it was never threatened even by the possibility of an airborne invasion by the Nazis. Apart from this, a Russian move to the western fringe of the continent, besides putting Russian bombers almost a thousand miles nearer our crowded Atlantic coast, would likewise give Russia possession of important natural resources and industrial skills: so that even if we were able to exterminate life completely in the heartland—a large if—we would still have to deal by purely military methods with the Russian seizure of Western Europe.

Soviet Russia already has the ironworks of Poland and Silesia and the munitions works of Czechoslovakia: tomorrow she may add the coal and iron resources of the Saar and Lorraine, to say nothing of Turin and Milan. In all these industries, there is a sufficient number of well-disciplined Communist workers to ensure a steady supply of weapons and goods. Would we, in this case, be ready to use instruments of mass extermination on the peoples of the West, too? That would only pyramid our lethal mistakes without increasing our safety; for, if thwarted in Europe, Russia would direct her efforts to China and India. With their talent for thriving under conditions of physical hardship and living off the land, the Russian armies could probably move farther and quicker in Asia than any force we could at once bring against them.

From this brief military survey certain facts should emerge: facts which, I suspect, have already become clear to our joint chiefs of staff.* The first is that our

* Plainly in 1948 I over-estimated the military sagacity of the Armed Forces. The Korean war caught them shamefully unprepared to intervene effectively in what should have been a minor conflict; and to the end they never made good our critical deficiencies in essential matters

confidence in the silver bullet tempted us to abandon too quickly the common lead variety. In our present situation, two million airborne troops, with sufficient planes to transport them anywhere at a week's notice, and with tanks and artillery equally mobile, would be far more useful than any conceivable quantity of atom bombs and bacteria, even if we had an unlimited number of swift bombers to carry them to their targets. Moreover, because of the loose, sprawling, amorphous structure of our enemy's homeland, his vulnerability to any kind of attack, even atomic attack, is far lower than our own: so that no matter with what striking successes an atomic war might begin, it would not be a brief war, neither would it be a cheap one. If we had enough instruments of genocide to make continental Russia uninhabitable—this is at least theoretically conceivable— we should also automatically bring disaster to the rest of the human race, including ourselves. As a result of the Bikini experiment, radioactive particles were detected within a week on our Pacific coast. So the atom bombs we cast on the enemy's waters would, like the Biblical bread, come back to us many-fold: but as a

like munitions. The present (1954) policy of "massive retaliation" shows that our leaders have learned nothing from Korea; nor have they yet acknowledged the painful fact that Soviet Russia's equal capacity for massive retaliation nullifies all the supposed advantages of our instruments of extermination.

curse, not a blessing. In short, a genuine war of extermination would bring about our own downfall. It would be no consolation, at the end, to remember that Russia had also lost everything.

Since 1946, the tension between the United States and Soviet Russia has grown acute. We should deceive ourselves if we failed to admit that our own errors have brought this about quite as much as the Kremlin's belligerence. Russia's conduct can be interpreted as the composite of three forces, each driving her in the same direction. The first is fear of the immediate effect of an atom bomb attack: a fear that will last until she has something like parity. This fear, incidentally, is not lessened by an article in the U. S. Air Force's *Air University Quarterly Review* * proving, on constitutional grounds, that such a surprise attack may be legally authorized by the President of the United States. The second force is hope: hope based on the supposition that our capitalist economy, following Marx's law, will presently collapse, more disastrously than in 1929, thereby leaving Russia as the receiver in bankruptcy of all the countries dependent on our aid. The third force, finally, is self-confidence: a confidence based on her

* Coira, Louis E., "Military Action Prior to Declaration of War," *Air University Quarterly Review* (Maxwell Field, Alabama). Vol. I, No. 3 (1947, Winter), pp. 66-78.

successful military repulse of Nazi Germany, and on the continued expansion of her own system of totalitarian control, with its centralized planning and disciplined party government. "Have we at least achieved Communism, Comrade, or will things get even worse?" That very joke points to the strength of the system.

But in certain particulars Russia's mistakes have been almost as disastrous as our own. For one thing, the Russians underestimated the effect of scarcity and depletion in maintaining American productivity during the postwar period: since we did not adopt the shortsighted policy of rapid deflation, even the unrestrained and merciless profiteering that took place did not act as a fatal brake on buying power. Further, the Russians forgot that since 1929 we had created a series of economic cushions, such as unemployment insurance, old-age pensions, steep income taxes, to say nothing of strong trade-union control, all of which have lessened the probability of a total economic collapse in the immediate future. Finally, the rigid ideological dogmatism of the Kremlin kept it from understanding that a system flexible enough, even before war broke out, to adopt such a noncapitalistic device as lend-lease might also be flexible enough to devise a Marshall Plan, which in the very act of helping to rehabilitate Europe would give an extra lease of life to our own mixed economy. Paradoxically, Russia's very truculence not merely guaranteed the passage of the European Recovery Act, but has added an extra prop to our economy by furthering our preparations for war: a guarantee against any sag in our heavy goods industries. Thanks to Russia's happy miscalculations some of our worst blunders have been partly rectified.

But does this mean that our new policy aimed at military balance will provide any better security than our concentration on weapons of extermination did? Not in the least. The dynamic part of Russian communism consists of a technique of terrorism, masked by an idea of human improvement; and ideas can be combatted only by better ideas. The significant idea behind communism is that of abolishing the exploitation of human beings through the private ownership of the means of production. Any nation or political group that hopes to achieve power and influence today must take this idea as its own starting point and show that there are better means of attaining it than through the technique of terrorism, suppression, and party control that Russia has so efficiently perfected. Against the monolithic economic system of the Russians we should oppose, not a fictitious version of our own economy in an equally monolithic form, but the actual pluralistic system which allows the greatest variety and play to whatever economic forces and institutions, private or public, will efficiently further the common good. In a country whose public education was free long before Russia's, we stultify ourselves and reduce our influence in other lands by pretending that we are governed only by the belief in private profit. If that were so, all our schools would be run privately, as they were in England early in the nineteenth century. Similarly, the TVA is as characteristic of our American economy as Du Pont or General Motors. To combat Russia's false ideology we must have something equally dynamic to give to the world; and we will awaken only jealousy, envy, and resentment if we associate our international policy with the forces of monopolistic capitalism at home and reactionary class interests abroad. Eventually, we must bring forth within the United Nations proposals for promoting the welfare of humanity as a whole which will make as much sense to the Russians as to ourselves. To contain Soviet Russia, we must include her.

In short, no purely military measures will give us the power to prevail over Russia's ideas or to avoid a final collision with those ideas on a field of battle. *If we continue to rely upon negative measures alone, we are headed straight for war, extermination, and the wholesale disintegration of modern civilization.* The fact is that both the United States and Soviet Russia have misconceived their national interests, and have acted as if one side or the other would absolutely prevail. Both are wrong. There is no way out of the present impasse which will not require painful sacrifice by ourselves as well as the Russians; for unless we contrive an honorable method to meet each other halfway we cannot continue to live in the same world. If we are to live together politically, Russia will have to abandon its fascist methods; for they are hostile to all the forces that enhance and develop human life. We, in our turn, will have to give up, not the institutions of democracy, but the notion that mammonism and mechanism are the be-all and end-all of human existence. So the next question is: on what basis, before it is too late, can the governments of both states retreat from the suicidal course they have been following? Countries that possess instruments of genocide must either bring about an Open World— the world symbolized by the air age—or perish within a closed world.

With these facts in mind, I present a series of proposals as a basis for immediate discussion and quick action. The underlying premise of these proposals is that they must without reserve be as significant and as hopeful to the people of Russia and the Communist-dominated countries as to the people of the United States and their allies. The program presented is mainly a combination of separate suggestions, put forward by different individuals and groups, but so far unconnected and unintegrated. If for brevity I put the succession of operations and proposals in a series of brusque propositions, it is not because I believe that, once the discussion is actively stated, still better suggestions may not be produced, but only because I believe that the facts themselves must be persuasive. If they are not, no eloquence or grace or modesty on the part of the present writer will bring about conviction.

Under ordinary circumstances, the first steps we should take, before war fever mounts higher, would involve heavy risk. So long as our negative policy persists, neither the armed forces nor the State Department could sanction them: at the moment I write our government seems even reluctant to guarantee eventual military support against Russian invasion. But the risk will be diminished almost to zero, if we immediately attach to our note of warning an honest plan of conciliation. Preliminary to this first proposal, in order to leave Soviet Russia in no doubt as to the consequences of her actions we should through our Chief Executive address the Soviet Government somewhat in the following manner:

The United States and Soviet Russia are already at war: we know that as well as you do. We do not propose to postpone facing the ultimate issues by further temporizing, withdrawal, or appeasement: that would only add heavier penalties to the final reckoning. Though you have so far won the opening moves of this war, we do not for a moment concede the possibility of your being victorious. But we do know that if the cold war became a hot one, both our countries would meet irreparable disaster and defeat. While we warn you that your next step toward subjugating, directly or indirectly, by political or by military means, any other country in Europe or Asia will be treated by us as an overt act of war, we beg you to pause long enough to consider the consequences. We have a selfish interest in asking you to stay your hand, because we know that war would work our ruin as well as yours. Confident of our own strength, determined to do our full share to head off this final catastrophe, we come to you now with a series of related proposals, for our common advantage.

First Proposal. Let us arrange a world armistice, limited to one year. During this year let us restrain every word, every gesture, every move that would convey hostility or belligerence. Let our armies remain where they are, or withdraw to their own territories. In American labor disputes, we have learned the value of a "cooling-off period." So long as we rattle arms at each other, neither side can hear the other speak; and neither is in a disposition to listen to the other. This armistice will erect an extra safeguard against an "incident" that would bring on a blind retaliation, as the blowing up of the battleship *Maine* in Havana harbor brought on the Spanish-American War. Above all, the purpose of this armistice is to create an atmosphere of tranquillity, sanity, and good will: such an atmosphere as has not existed between the Western powers and Soviet Russia since the very birth of the Soviet Union. We suggest the time limit of one year in order to insure that both sides will direct their utmost efforts toward arriving at our common goal, security and peace, without rousing the suspicion that further delay might mean, for the other party, some new military advantage.

We attach to this plea for an armistice a *Second Proposal:* also by way of preparation. We believe that no immediate meeting of our representatives will succeed, so long as they carry into that meeting the convictions, the attitudes, and the fixed ideas they have brought to all the other conferences. We believe it is possible to transform these rigid attitudes—though not without risks to our respective ideologies—by showing that neither totalitarianism nor democracy, communism nor free enterprise, can hope to survive a war of extermination. Unless we are full of blind hatred for humanity itself, like Hitler and his followers, that fact must give us both pause.

84

This thesis, we believe, is open to demonstration. To this end we suggest that you join us in inviting the United Nations to take part in an honest, impartial inquiry into the nature of the "total war" we have both been preparing. Our purpose is to arrive at an objective assessment of its certain consequences to our own countries and to mankind at large. At present all the resources of science are being used to create new forms of extermination, without the slightest public effort being made to apply a scientific prognosis to the results. We believe that only the truth, the whole truth, and nothing but the truth can save us from the hideous forces we now have unleashed.

Once the struggle between our countries becomes intense, we shall both resort to mass extermination on the widest scale. Do you doubt it? We can deduce what means you may use: we *know* our own capacities. There is no defense against genocide by countergenocide: the only possible form of security is the conquest and complete occupation of the country practicing it; and for either of us to effect that end, we should have to have every other major power in the world as our active ally. In a singlehanded fight we would practice unlimited destruction and extermination without coming a step nearer that goal.

As to American capacities for mass extermination, we shall spare you any guesswork on these matters: we propose at this world conference to lift all restrictions of military security, so-called, in order to make known the actual number of atom bombs we now possess, their deadliness in terms of those we dropped on Japan, and our productive capacity in all *other* instruments of genocide. We will make public the means we now possess for poisoning air and water and soil on a scale that will ultimately exterminate life in every form. You may check our conclusions with your own scientists and with their colleagues in other countries. Since this conference seeks to lay bare the data on which rational conclusions about the safety and welfare of the human race must be drawn, we suggest that it take the form of a world congress of scientists, particularly nuclear physicists, chemists, bacteriologists, geneticists, ecologists: people whose conclusions, if anything like unanimous, would have final authority. Day by day, they would reveal the essential facts, interpret them, and assess them. Mankind would listen.

At present, all this knowledge is subdivided, secret, inviolable, remote from all but the most casual public scrutiny: hence every action we are preparing to take is, even for our highest government officers, a leap in the dark. We propose to provide the necessary data—hoping all other countries will do the same—that will enable the scientists concerned to estimate, quantitatively, the deadliness of the weapons we now possess: likewise the increasing ratio of danger as time goes on. Within two months, once secrecy is lifted, we are confident that the facts can be brought together and weighed, and the inevitable conclusions drawn. Such a period, therefore, would be more than a cooling-off period, in which frustrations and angers would be erased and self-control and mutual respect established. This period, for the other nations of the world as well as ourselves, would be dedicated to bringing about a profound moral change: such a complete transformation as took place during those memorable days of the French Revolution when the feudal estates of France, voluntarily and almost overnight, renounced all their ancient feudal privileges.

We grant that the difficulties are great: *both our countries must change their minds;* and that will be a harder task for you than for ourselves, since during the last decade the peoples of Britain and the United States have come to understand the interdependence of mankind: former isolationists like our Senator Vandenberg became the foremost advocates of world co-operation. We have further steps in mind to make your own reversal of policy easier. But to carry this change through, it is important that your political representatives and ours should attend this congress of scientists day by day, and that our peoples should have a complete daily report of all the proceedings. This will be a day of judgment for all of us: perhaps a Last Judgment on our civilization.

What would the conclusions of such a conference be? An American can perhaps anticipate them with more readiness than his Russian opposite number; for these conclusions have already been stated for us by men not lacking in military skill, in manly self-confidence, or in patriotism. Generals MacArthur and Arnold have both said that *There will be no victor in World War III*. Behind their judgment as soldiers stands an overwhelming mass of scientific evidence. We rely upon that evidence, once it is fully exposed, to effect a change of heart and mind in every government and in every people, a change capable of making them uproot their fixed ideas, mollify their hostilities, and stimulate the processes of co-operation. Without such a change, the next series of proposals would face insurmountable barriers. With a sufficient change, we can go forward with the main business in hand.

Only with some such beginning can we hope for success in undertaking more positive measures. One must assume, as the basis for possible success, that the rulers of Soviet Russia, though they will have serious difficulty in giving up their dogmatic suppositions and prejudgments, are as capable as we are of acting on honest

88

evidence—provided that they realize that every alternative door, which might let them bolster their power without demanding any closer co-operation with the democratic nations, is closed. The conference that assesses the possibilities of genocide will in fact close every door but one: the door to World Government.

The *Third Proposal,* then, is that Soviet Russia and the United States take the initiative in transforming the dummy model of the United Nations, which is a disguise for a feeble confederation of independent sovereign states, into an effective working machine: a complete system of world government. To do this every nation will have to relinquish part of its sovereignty and initiative in all matters of common concern to the rest of mankind: in particular, to surrender the implements for making war, to a central governmental authority, capable of instituting justice and effectually maintaining peace. Without this proviso for guarding minorities, equalizing burdens, removing grievances, no suppression of arms will be effective and no lasting peace will be possible. Whatever illusions people have nourished till now, there is *no halfway point* along the road to world co-operation at which we may safely stop: we cannot by degrees add powers to mechanisms originally designed to remain inert and powerless. Today it is a question of All or Nothing. Unless we establish a world government capable of creating an *Open World,* with an ever-freer movement of men, goods, and ideas across all national boundaries, we cannot even create an inspection force large enough to insure against secret forms of rearmament and genocide. Every national must be, of right, a citizen of the world, and while retaining every local social affection and loyalty, his highest allegiance must be to humanity.

Will Soviet Russia, which now belligerently resists co-operations of the most tentative kind, even refusing to join UNESCO, take this gigantic step? Before the conference on genocide, the odds would be heavily against this happening. But once Soviet Russia had agreed to the armistice and had made a careful calculation of the ultimate results of mass extermination, if the cold war became a hot one, the situation would be far more favorable to a decisive reorientation in Russian policy, even if that brought on a change of Russian leadership. To make this reorientation easier, the United States should underline the peaceful intent of all our proposals by concrete actions the nature of which would leave no doubts in Russia's mind. At this point, it is hardly possible to appraise the potentialities of enlisting Russia's support for world government without reading and pondering G. A. Borgese's brilliant exposition of "What to Do with Russia" in *Common Cause* (October, November, and

December, 1947). In the current proposals I am doing little more than attaching Mr. Borgese's general theme to a more specific series of objectives.

Fourth Proposal: To prove our good faith in taking the lead for world government, a good faith that the Russians may continue to doubt, we should meet them more than halfway. Secure in the existence of our present military machine, enlarged, we hope, to meet every demand of classic warfare, the next gesture, however generous, would involve no direct military risk that would not be easily reparable. Even before the United Nations is transformed into world government, before adequate inspection measures can be devised and put into operation, we should cease manufacturing atom bombs and other instruments of extermination. As soon as Soviet Russia indicates a willingness to accept world government, with all that it implies by way of democratic procedure, we should dismantle our atom bombs, destroy our biological weapons, and forgo any further production of atomic energy until this can be handled by a world authority.

So much for a program designed to lessen Russia's suspicion and hostility, and to create a confidence that would make possible equally firm measures of co-operation on her part. But we should re-enforce these measures, again voluntarily, by taking the initiative for world

91

justice, creating a pattern which will be followed more comprehensively by world government, once it is in working order. Pursuing Mr. Grenville Clark's wise suggestions, we should meet Russia's demand for control over the Dardanelles by declaring our willingness at once to place *all* international straits and canals under United Nations administration; and in advance of a plan for rationing energies and primary resources, we should extend the Bernard Baruch proposals for a World Control of Atomic Energy to other essential resources: petroleum, say.

If American statesmanship makes world co-operation its *prime* objective, we must realize that both the Baruch Plan and the Marshall Plan, like Lend-Lease before them, cannot be considered as purely temporary expedients, designed to bolster a disintegrating world economy. Quite the contrary, they must be known as the corner-stones of a post-imperialist economy, designed to transform a world based on the one-sided exploitation of the weak by the strong, with each economic group, each national state, intent on private advantage, into a co-operative commonwealth of the nations, spending prudently on peace what they have hitherto spent so recklessly on war, sharing abundance instead of destroying it, forgoing temporary profits for durable human welfare. In terms of a world organized to produce peace, national monopolies and exclusive rights of exploitation do not make sense. "The earth is the Lord's and the fullness thereof": this is no longer a hollow dictum of religion but a directive for economic action toward human brotherhood.

No single action that the United States might take belligerently in opposition to Russia would so effectively undermine the Russian aggression and hostility, or break down the ideological case Russia has built up against us in the minds of the poor and exploited countries of the world, than the announcement of our willingness to participate in a system of world resource rationing, as a condition of establishing a world government. In a single stroke, we should transform the Kremlin's powerful ideological sword into a shattered icicle. Put forward in good faith and backed by appropriate acts, such a policy would disarm Communist belligerence more effectively than any quantity of lethal weapons. The appeal would be addressed, not to governments but to the peoples living under communism, who are as eager as the western democracies to live in peace.

Behind all these proposals is a simple fact, effectively stated by Professor Borgese: any plans for coming together with Russia instead of fighting her must envisage objectives and goals which make sense in terms of her ideal purposes as well as ours. We cannot create an effective world government if we think merely in terms of containing communism; nor shall we provide for peace and security if at the outset we give up the hope of including Russia in this larger system of unity. In a world organized for peace, capitalism and communism may both, in a limited sense, survive: *but they cannot hope to exist side by side on their own exclusive terms without undergoing any further change.* If the logic of events forces Soviet Russia to accept, against all her historic traditions, continuous from Ivan the Terrible to Stalin and Malenkov, the unfamiliar methods of Western democracy, which world government necessitates, the same logic also applies to the United States: we must accept and further that tendency toward the equalization of economic privileges and advantages which the conservative de Tocqueville identified with the rise of democracy itself.

In neither national nor international life has that equalization process reached its terminus; but the fact is that it has gone much further in democratic England, our closest partner, than in Soviet Russia. Now a progressive equalization of wealth between nations is one of the substantial promises of world government: indeed, our more farsighted industrialists understand by now that it is the foundation even for a healthy national economy. If we lack the political intelligence to go along with this movement and to direct it we shall become the target of the world's envy, jealousy, hatred: on those terms, we shall turn the world over to Soviet Russia, until both systems resort to mass extermination: alias "war." All this means that world government imposes sacrifices and burdens: burdens that will bear most heavily on ourselves. But however steep the price of world government, if considered in annual contributions of taxes on a basis of national wealth, it will be picayune compared to the costs of a third world war. Every canvass of alternatives must be calculated on that basis. If our house is likely to be burned to the ground, a heavy insurance premium is cheaper than the bill for replacement.

There are certain current habits of mind that stand in the way of giving these proposals serious consideration.

The first is the fallacy of gradualism: the notion that every change must be approached by slow degrees, and that the preatomic form of the United Nations may, by a succession of minor modifications, become strong enough to carry the load of world peace. Actually, the United Nations has been weakened, not strengthened, by time. Not merely has the succession of Russian vetoes flouted the authority of the majority, but even worse the United States, by its withdrawal of its own proposal for partitioning Palestine, has robbed the organization of its last vestige of dignity and power. Any organization that reverses its decision at the first hint of rebellion by a handful of hostile Arabs cannot, plainly, overcome the continental belligerence of the United States and Soviet Russia. We have no time to build a bridge across the deep chasm between the East and the West: hand in hand, Soviet Russia and the United States must both take a leap. But if one has to jump across a six-foot chasm one must go all the way: a two-foot jump will merely insure a broken neck.*

The second obstructive habit of mind derives from the notion that if only the present showdown can be postponed, some yet undetected agent will save us from the final catastrophe. So people kept on hoping during the period when Hitler, like Stalin and Malenkov, moved triumphantly on the path of "peaceful" aggression and domination; and despite the fact that history has completely discredited the Chamberlains and the Borahs and the Beards, their ghosts go marching on. In view of the fact that the instruments of genocide will become vastly more devastating, the sooner a peaceful show-

---

* Whether the United Nations has been weakened or strengthened by time is a difficult question even now to answer. Continued attempts to by-pass its procedures, to take unilateral measures, to evade its responsibilities plainly weaken it. On the other hand, the increase in the powers of the General Assembly, at the expense of the Security Council, beginning with the Korean decision, was a sign of health. My judgment here was impatient and faulty.

down takes place the better: provided that we bring to
the occasion positive plans and blueprints which will
bring about a constructive resolution of our difficulties.
*Unless our political or social inventions are equal to our
scientific and technological inventions, we confess complete intellectual and moral bankruptcy.*

Finally, there is a kind of mental block which takes
the form of saying: Politics is the "science of the possible," and these proposals are not within the realm of
the possible. By this, those who take this position mean
that any proposal which involves difficulties and sacrifices of a greater order than people normally accept
must be carefully kept from view, in order to spare the
feelings of all concerned. But if the experience of the
last ten years proves anything, this platitude is as empty
as it is mealy-mouthed. In terms of the "science of the
possible" England should have surrendered to Germany
between July, 1940 and June, 1941. Actually England
was saved (and the world was saved, too) because
Churchill told the English not what they would have
liked to hear, but what they needed to hear in order to
bear the day's burden: he told them that their lot would
be all but insupportable and that he could promise nothing in the way of immediate victory: nothing, indeed,
except that they were about to live through their finest
hour. If politics means anything today it must become

the "art of the *im*possible." The people who sacrifice every principle to expediency, every long-range plan to immediate profit, every hope of world government to maneuvering for position in a war that will bring about the extirpation of democracy and the disintegration of human society—it is these people who live in a world of slippery fantasies and self-deceptions. In terms of the "possible" we have only two courses open: suicide by appeasement or suicide by war. The "impossible" is world government and world co-operation: the road to life.

Not for a moment would I underestimate the psychological revolution that will have to take place before these proposals can be seriously considered. At the present moment, the chances for such a program as I have outlined being put forward within the next year are something less, I should judge, than one in a hundred; for the conceptions they are based on are foreign to most of our present leaders in both parties. Mr. Justice Douglas alone has spoken along these general lines. These ideas, indeed, might more easily come from one of our military leaders than from any visible politician. Day by day, however, the issues become grimmer and the dangers more horrifying: once all the tempting irrational exits are closed, one must hope that the door indicated by reason and common sense will finally open.

That "miracle" is the only alternative to catastrophe. But we must not wait for catastrophe before we acknowledge its possibility.

On this matter, if one cannot be an optimist, one dare not be a pessimist. In the utter hopelessness and panic of the depression in 1933, the audacious measures undertaken by the Roosevelt administration, often in contradiction to pre-election commitments, restored public confidence, encouraged enterprise, and brought about production, through hitherto unthinkable uses of public credit and public aid to the unemployed. That, in its way, was a miracle: comparable to the one needed today. So again, with the transformation of the skeptical, cynical, debunked, mainly pacifist younger generation of Americans into tough fighters who beat the Nazis at their own game: what was that, whether viewed as a technical or a moral achievement, if not a gigantic miracle? No change that these young men underwent to prepare themselves for combat is harder than that we must now collectively make under equally dire compulsion, in order to lay the foundations for peace.

The miracle of stopping our present war with Russia and averting total catastrophe is still within human scope. It will require intelligence, imagination, and audacity, all on a heroic scale: but by no means of a superhuman order. These qualities exist in every country. Let us put them to work before it is too late.

V

MIRRORS OF VIOLENCE

When the nineteenth century was coming to an end, a hot argument broke out as to whether the date 1900 marked the beginning of the twentieth century or the last year of the old. One might again provoke a similar debate in discussing the literature of the last fifty years, were it not for the fact that we now realize that the dates on the calendar must all be shifted.

We know, to begin with, that the nineteenth century began in 1815 and that it came to an end not in 1901 but in 1914. As for what has happened since, we have condensed time in the very fashion Henry Adams predicted. In thirty years we have encompassed as many terrible changes as the Romans did between the period of the Antonines and the foundation of the Benedictine Order.

No one can understand the literature of the last half century, its contradictions, its dehumanization, its preoccupation with violence, its increasing unintelligibility, who does not understand the great breach that World War I effected in the human mind. While our visible monuments are still continuous with those of the nineteenth century, all our invisible landmarks have been defaced or demolished: "Over is under and close is apart." We were born into the cocky, confident world of Bernard Shaw; and we have lived to understand sympathetically the plight and confessions of Saint Augustine. To interpret the literature of our period, we must realize how time has been distorted for us by the meeting, within a generation, of still youthful senescents and grimly senescent youths: it is the old who are giddy and the young who are grave.

Before World War I the greater part of Western Civilization was still inflated by the profound optimism that had buoyed up the nineteenth century, the Century of Progress. Under the influence of the new ideology that had grown up with capitalism and mechanical invention, the leading minds of the period thought that mankind had found the secret of happiness by turning its attention to the quantitative solution of all its problems. The ultimate enigmas of man's nature and destiny no longer plagued these leaders: they could bury their doubts in productive work. Confused by the word, they sought certainty in the deed. "In the beginning," said Goethe, turning his back on the Gospel of St. John, "was the act." "Let us act that each tomorrow finds us farther than today," urged Longfellow. "Let us work," said

101

Chekhov's Uncle Vanya, fleeing from frustration, boredom, and morphine. In those three sentences the resolute pragmatism of the nineteenth century could be summed up.

On these premises, utopia seemed just around the corner; and perhaps the most influential book of the late nineteenth century, which expressed most deeply its hopes and aspirations, was Edward Bellamy's *Looking Backward*. At the turn of the century H. G. Wells wrote a postscript, called in its full title *Anticipations of the Reaction of Mechanical and Scientific Progress*. Both books were written out of a genuine insight into the technical achievements of modern culture; and if these new elements alone had been operative, our age might have steadily extended its physical comforts and nourished its spiritual complacency, in widening waves of "pneumatic bliss." These thinkers hardly anticipated that all our rational devices might fall into the hands of irrational men.

Now there was still another book that caused much controversy at the end of the nineteenth century: Max Nordau's study, *Degeneration*. That book was full of atrocious juxtapositions and erroneous generalizations, so it cannot be recommended, any more than Spengler's later study of the downfall of the West, as a work of impeccable scholarship. But the reaction against it was not due simply to Nordau's loose thinking: it was due to the general belief that degeneration was impossible in the literature or art produced by a Century of Progress.

Did not the law of Progress hold everywhere? Reviewing Tennyson's poetry, John Stuart Mill—or was it Macaulay?—had observed that it was as natural to anticipate that the mechanism of a nineteenth-century poem should be better than the crude form of a ballad, as that the mechanism of a cotton mill should be better than a hand loom. Nordau scandalously suggested the opposite; worse, he held that the leading writers and artists of the period were neurotic men, prophets and exponents of disintegration.

If the shoddy evidence Nordau brought forward did not confirm his judgment—he even cited the impressionists, those pure and healthy spirits, to prove how painting had degenerated!—he had, perhaps by accident, a curiously sound intuition of the future. In time, the most sensitive spirits of the twentieth century confirmed his apprehensions, not about their personal degeneration but about certain cancerous growths within our society, attitudes and beliefs that made possible war and destruction and torture and Fascist slavery on a scale that had once been unthinkable.

Henry Adams as historian, James Joyce as novelist,

T. S. Eliot as poet, looking into their souls, found a different picture from Wells's *Anticipations*. True, the smooth motor roads, the flying planes, the automatic factories, had all duly arrived; but what the new writers discovered, long before the events themselves were visible, was corruption, confusion, delirium, babble, violence, and death. These themes began to appear, with increasing frequency, in those writers whose creative gifts were most indisputable: in Hermann Hesse and Thomas Mann in Germany, in Marcel Proust and André Gide in France, in Joyce and Eliot and Lawrence in England; in Hemingway, Faulkner, and Waldo Frank in the United States.

Once the furor over Nordau's book died down, it had no influence; yet all that he said about the neurotic qualities of modern art and the modern sensibility was carried further by another physician whose thoughts were to dominate the first half of our century, Dr. Sigmund Freud. With Freud the center of intellectual gravity shifted from the external world to the internal world, from the objective to the subjective, from the stable common sense of Trollope and Dickens and Tolstoy to the demonic world of the dream, a world spawning monsters that the rationalists of the nineteenth century thought science had destroyed forever. The mission of Freud was to create a psychology of depth, on the basis of his original *Interpretation of Dreams*. He brought to light the dark underworld of the unconscious, proved that every symbol and image was significant, and revealed how shallow the structure of Victorian common sense had been.

If the world of the nineteenth century was mainly a daylight world, reveling in clear vistas and distant prospects, the world of the early twentieth century was a nighttime world, a world of deep instinctual urges and explosive emotions, newly conscious, through Freud and Havelock Ellis, of a sexuality that no longer found an easy channel in profuse fertility and kindly family life. The optimists of the machine had forgotten that there was night and madness and mystery to contend with, coexisting with daylight and science and universal literacy. Because they had forgotten the darker side of man's nature, they were spiritually unprepared for the catastrophes that have actually marked this half century.

Herman Melville had written, in *Clarel*, that we were "but drilling the new Hun, whose growl even now can some dismay"; and Burckhardt, most penetrating of historians, had predicted the coming of the Terrible Simplifiers, people who would simplify physics, to remove the Jewish element, like Hitler and the Nobel physicist, Lennard; or who would simplify history in order to erase the names of comrades they had liquidated, like Stalin. But who among the more popular writers of the twentieth century had anticipated the possibilities of the torture chamber and the extermination camp? World War I was a dividing point. Before it came, in one of the best of his novels, *The New Machiavelli*, Wells had presented his hero boasting, in exile, "No King, no Council, can seize me or torture me; no Church, no nation, can silence me—such powers of ruthless and complete suppression have vanished."

Within twenty years that boast had become hollow and that security unthinkable. The Machine, by which I mean all the agencies of order, regularity, and efficiency, whether social or technical, had itself suddenly become irrational. In Russia the social revolution, which had issued out of a generous dream of human freedom, promoted a despotism more ruthless than that of the czars; in America, with the depression, an excess of mechanical production produced only poverty, bankruptcy, and despair. On the surface it would seem that this disrupted age might have atoned for its miscarried idealisms and its abortive revolutions by enabling the writer to bring back into literature the whole man, in all his dimensions, now that his impulses and hidden motives had been revealed. Had not the whole man been almost forgotten in a period that had attempted to identify human capacities and interests with the glossy

106

externalism and inhuman perfections of the Machine? But the results were not quite so simple or so fortunate. If the Victorian myth in America was concerned mainly with costume and setting, the twentieth-century myth merely reversed this process. The new myth found its way into the dark interior and forgot the saving humanities and sanities that penetrated even this darkness. So the twentieth century created a sort of inverted hypocrisy, substituting blackened for whited sepulchers, a hypocrisy that deferentially acknowledged the forces of darkness and denied those of light. Instead of the whole man, our writers have created only a Surrealist Man, disemboweled like a Dali figure, kicking his own severed head across a blasted landscape. Certainly, the whole man is not included in the popular tallies of the Naked and the Dead, from John Dos Passos to Norman Mailer.

As interpreters of our time, our best writers have done justice to the forces that undermine us and debase us, and it is a nice question whether, in their act of revelation, they are helping to lance the abscess that threatens us or have themselves merely added to the mass of morbid tissue. But if contemporary literature altogether satisfied our spiritual needs, if it were wholly representative of our aspirations and pointed adequately to the future, one could hardly account for the revival of interest in the world of Henry James, a world where reason, in the form of the artist's conscience, is constantly in command, delicately probing, making swift incisions, but always limiting the scope of its operations to those situations where human insight and skill remain uppermost; not a profound or heroic world, but one in which all the healthy living functions are still active.

James is the historic representative in our generation of those men of letters who purchase wholeness by withdrawal from the life that might injure them. Such encapsulated writers—Joseph Conrad, Robert Frost, Rainer Maria Rilke—strong enough to oppose their time's decay, great enough to continue growth within self-imposed limitations that wall them against further disintegration, do not create a new vision of life, but they remind their contemporaries that wholeness is still possible. Their influence today hopefully modifies the dark picture, though their very insulation keeps them from actively changing it.

Analyzing the popular novels of our decade and country, one of our most perceptive psychologists has discovered, as the dominating attitude of their writers, self-contempt and disgust. They write without love of a life that is unlovable. Even the more significant writers of our time have not altogether escaped the danger of being overpowered by the corrupt nature of their material: note the contrast between Mann's *The Magic Mountain*, which remains healthy though constantly preoccupied with disease, and his *Doctor Faustus*, which deals with creativity but is unfavorably affected by the hero's own disintegration. Yet plainly our writers have at least discovered, in man's own lower depths, the forces that have brought on the series of catastrophes that have marked our time—the fighting of two wars on a planetary scale, the restoration of torture and slavery, the extermination of between seventeen and eighteen million Nazi victims, six million of them Jews, and the overnight destruction of whole cities under the guise of "strategic bombing," practiced by an enemy we have yet to confront accusingly in the mirror—ourselves.

If our civilization is not to produce greater holocausts, our writers will have to become something more than merely mirrors of its violence and disintegration; they, through their own efforts, will have to regain the initiative for the human person and the forces of life, chaining up the demons we have allowed to run loose, and releasing the angels and ministers of grace we have shamefacedly—and shamefully—incarcerated. For the writer is still a maker, a creator, not merely a recorder of fact, but above all an interpreter of possibilities. His intuitions of the future may still give body to a better world and help start our civilization on a fresh cycle of adventure and effort. The writer of our time must find within himself the wholeness that is now lacking in his society. He must be capable of interpreting life in all its dimensions, particularly in the dimensions the last half century has neglected; restoring reason to the irrational, purpose to the defeatists and drifters, value to the nihilists, hope to those sinking in despair.

We cannot possibly know at what date the first half of the twentieth century will actually end, for that ending will be a spiritual event not recorded by the calendar. Yet we can predict one of the events that may well mark it: the appearance of a novel or a poem or a play or even a philosophic work in which the whole man will become visible, as visible as the disintegrated man of our time in *Ulysses* or *The Remembrance of Things Past*. This still-unborn—or unrecognized—creature will focus in himself all the healing forces that are still present in our society: he will help us to transcend, first in a new attitude of mind and spirit and then in effective actions, the catastrophes that now widely threaten mankind.

VI

RENEWAL IN THE ARTS

In every part of our civilization today, to take a look at
the situation from the highest possible vantage point,
it is plain to all who are sufficiently awakened, at least,
that mankind is on the brink of a great change; though
we do not know yet whether that change will save our
present civilization from an all but final catastrophe, or
enable our descendants to pick up the pieces afterward,
as the transformation of classic Roman culture into
Christianity enabled the survivors of the Dark Ages to
rebuild their lives on a different plan. To a generation
that has been bred on the notion of change, and that has
even, with John Dewey's followers, largely defined education as adaptation to change, this may not seem a particularly new situation. But there is something new in the
present posture of things; and this is the fact that a
change sufficient to ward off or overcome the catastrophes
that now threaten the world will involve a radical breach
and discontinuity with the changes that have taken place
during the last three centuries. It will, first of all, be an
inner change, a change of direction and purpose, not

111

just a change of speed and quantity; and instead of being based on the continued conquest of nature, it will be based on the restoration and the renewal of man— that poor bewildered creature, man, who in our day has become an impoverished exile, a displaced person cut off both from his native land he has left and from a new world that refuses to recognize his existence.

This change in the direction of our civilization has long been overdue; and the proof that it is overdue lies in the wholesale miscarriage of human hopes and plans that has taken place during the last fifty years: a miscarriage that has caused the Century of Progress, as people fondly called the nineteenth century, to give way to half a century of savage regression. I need hardly call to your minds the too-familiar proofs of this fact. In a brief thirty years, punctuated by two world wars and a series of almost equally grisly revolutions, we have prematurely wiped out between forty and fifty million lives, on the most conservative calculation. We now begin to realize, perhaps, why the very signs that the nineteenth century took as proofs of inevitable progress—"men shall run to and fro and knowledge shall be increased"—were taken by the writer of the Book of Daniel as a sign of the last days. The fact is that it is not ignorance and poverty and weakness, those old enemies of man, that threaten Western Civilization; just the reverse: it is knowledge of godlike dimensions, wealth on a scale that mankind has never enjoyed before, and power of the most titanic order, all the goals Western man has pursued so single-mindedly the last three centuries, that have brought this civilization to the brink of disintegration.

Patently that road has not merely proved a blind alley: it may well be a death trap. If we move further along that road, we shall be fatally caught: hence the task of our generation is to retrace our steps, to reorient ourselves, and to discover alternative courses. We must re-examine man's needs and re-establish more human goals than those we have mistakenly pursued: we must choose the road to life, which of old was called the road to salvation, and which now is also the road to survival. We need more knowledge still, but of a different kind from the fragmentary, unco-ordinated triumphs of modern specialists; we need more wealth, but a wealth measured in terms of life rather than profit and prestige; we need more power, too, the human power to control, to inhibit, to direct, to restrain, to withhold, in direct proportion to our augmented physical power to explode and destroy.

These words may well fall with an ominous sound on the ears of a generation schooled to look upon all changes as progressive, upon all mechanical inventions as desirable, upon all inhibitions and controls as frustrating; people who, even when they were not Marxists, regarded history and culture as a sort of assembly-line process, in which man himself could play no decisive part, except possibly to accelerate further the inevitable movement of impersonal forces. Such people used to sum up that strange conviction by saying: You cannot turn the hands of the clock backward. But as a matter of demonstrable fact, that is neither practically nor metaphorically true. Our generation has repeatedly seen the hands of the clock turned backward for evil and villainous purposes, purposes that have made slavery and the butchery of innocent people commonplaces of totalitarian government; and this horrible negative example should convince us that the hands of the clock may be turned backward, perhaps, for good purposes too, provided that sane good men, who believe in the democratic and rational processes, know their minds as well as the brutal and demented ones do.

So, instead of furthering the present processes of automatism, instead of submitting to a love-denying and life-strangling routine, our hope lies in restoring to the very center of the mechanical world the human personality, now lost and bewildered and hungry in the jungle of mechanisms it has created. Where our ancestors sought power alone, we must seek control; where

114

our predecessors were interested only in causes and means, we must become equally interested in purposes and goals. That is why art and religion and ethics have a significance for the present generation that they did not enjoy even a decade ago; and that is why the arts themselves, precisely because they are among the central expressions of the personality, have a peculiar importance in helping us to understand our present predicament and to find a way out of it.

It is against this broad general background that I should like to place the more immediate problems of our time. Already, through the artists, we begin to catch a gleam, if only from a distance, of new manifestations of life, warmed by a humanity we were almost ashamed to confess, guided by ideals that had long been deflated and cast aside. If the changes we have been discussing were only a minor eddy, only a passing fashion, it is probable that the mood of the new generation, with its fresh respect for the traditional, the classical, the intelligible, the communicable, with its acceptance of ethical norms and civic responsibilities, with its unabashed embracement of emotions it had hitherto concealed as if shameful—if these changes were only on the surface, they would probably be followed by another outbreak of revolt. But if a much more sweeping redirection of human life actually impends, then perhaps the new movement will become even more central, because it will help, in time, to redefine the nature of the creative act, and will, by example, unite men in a common effort to make the expression of love and beauty, significance and order, the core of all human endeavor. In a somewhat weakly retrospective, if not reactionary, form, we have long seen this change taking place in older writers like Aldous Huxley and T. S. Eliot, who were among the first to explore the bleak Waste Land of the soul left at the end of World War I. The younger artists are now carrying their example even farther, in taking a more responsible attitude toward their audience; in accepting, in the spirit of Sophocles, the arduous duties of citizenship, and in cleaving to the great ethical issues of our time, they will in turn find their intuitive attitudes confirmed by a more conscious formulation of our common problem.

For the last three centuries Western man has been remolding his outer and his inner world with the aid of the machine, and increasingly in the image of the machine; in his preoccupation with the conquest of nature, he has unhappily lost sight of the human, the cosmic, and the divine. The ultimate source of this change was, without doubt, the scientific revolution that took place in the seventeenth century, a reaction against the tendency of the Christian church to identify its own limited

116

human province with the omniscience and the omnipotence it postulated for its God. Science, turning its back
upon the claims of Christian theology to have direct
revelation of all knowledge significant to man, occupied
itself with the piecemeal examination of external nature.
In the effort to achieve verifiable knowledge, science isolated quantities from qualities, objective data from subjective data, the measurable from the incommensurable,
the simple part from the complex whole. By that act
science thrust aside as unreal the world of the artist: the
world arising out of emotion and desire, the world of
the qualitative and the subjective, the world whose complex patterns become meaningless as soon as they are
reduced to mere fragments.

This deliberate depersonalization and dehumanization of knowledge gave the physical scientist a great
tool for reinvestigating the forces of nature; but at the
same time it reduced half of human life, the subjective
half, the inner half, to a state of insignificance, if not
actual nonexistence. Naturally enough, those who
brought about this change did not fully understand what
they were doing; like Descartes they even hid this heresy
from their own eyes by consigning the soul to the Church,
while everything they regarded as of rational importance
they reserved for science. But in the course of three centuries marked by the increasing intellectual and practi-

cal achievements of the physical sciences, the ultimate results of Galileo's original formulation of the procedures of science became, at long last, fully visible: science has not merely eliminated a thousand irrelevant fantasies and wishful projections that had kept man from understanding the nature of the physical world; but it also has undermined man himself, and all but eliminated from every department of life the essential concepts of purpose, value, and quality.

Man's autonomous inner world, the impulses and urges he projects and realizes in the forms of art, were foreign to science and completely irrelevant to its aims. In the ideal world that the scientist was creating, machines increasingly took the place of men, and men themselves were tolerated only to the extent that they took on the attributes of machines, free from passion and emotion, indifferent to values, unconcerned with any ends except those derived from the immediate job or process. Since man is himself part of the order of nature, he learned much about his own nature and his circumstances from this new method of thought; but at the same time he forgot many truths about his constitution and aptitudes that religion and art had always abundantly recognized. Only in the final stages of mechanization, the stage we are now entering, could the essential nature of what went before be fully discerned;

118

and it was not until our own day that the artist fully surrendered to the forces that, in the end, were to overwhelm the human personality. Before that happened, the artist, in fact, fought a long, rear-guard action against the encroachments of the machine.

The banner under which this rear-guard fight was waged was that of Romanticism; an attempt to reassert the validity of the organic, as against the mechanical, of the individual personality as against the statistical aggregate, of the instinctual and traditional and historical as against the purely rational and measurable. Those who served under this banner were plainly unfit to take part in the grand march of science and invention; and they fell quickly out of the procession—the Rousseaus who denied that man had improved under civilization, the Blakes who passionately denounced "single vision and Newton's sleep," the Ruskins who hated the dark relentless mills of the new industry, the Hugos and Dostoevskis and Tolstois, the Delacroixs and the Van Goghs, who proclaimed that the new civilization coming into existence under the impetus of science, capitalism, and mechanical invention was actually working to produce barbarism of the most inhuman and damnable sort.

Whereas the poet and artist had served willingly, yes joyfully, under the Christian Church, even during periods when it was most inimical to fresh thoughts and

119

feelings, there was scarcely an outstanding talent after the middle of the eighteenth century who was unqualifiedly on the side of the new forces: even poets like Emerson and Whitman, who most readily accepted the machine and hoped most from the applications of science, counterpoised that acceptance by a new demand for the personal. Whitman uttered that demand, with great clarity, in his *Democratic Vistas*, and even provided a grand outline of the new personalism that was to become the crown and justification of all the inordinate material triumphs of the nineteenth century. At the same time, the darker alternatives were equally clear. In his *Letters from the Underground*, Dostoevski's Hitlerian spokesman actually prophesied that if man continued on the path that seemed, to the nineteenth century, the "inevitable" and the progressive one, the human spirit, if it could not assert itself in any other way, would do so by crime, in deliberate outbreaks of torture and sadism, rather than in sweetness and light. Dostoevski saw, with what now almost seems clairvoyance, that the cult of the machine, pushed to the extremes of impersonality, might summon up from the depths of the human unconscious the demonic and the primitive: elements of violence and irrationality that would bring the whole structure toppling to the ground.

Those prophetic observations perhaps give us an in-

sight into why in practical life the country that had
exploited to the fullest degree the sources of science,
Germany, turned so easily to the irrationalities of *Führer*
worship and the infamy of the extermination camps;
just as, in the realm of art, it perhaps explains why the
wholly depersonalized art of the Cubists and the Su-
prematists was followed by the largely infantile or
neurotic art of the Surrealists, since it was only in the
private world of the unconscious that the human personality still maintained a foothold. From that vantage
point, while it could no longer control life, it could
make obscene sallies into the public world and at least
call attention to the personality's existence by commit-
ting a nuisance.

The rear-guard action of the Romanticists was a losing one: year by year, they were forced to give up more
ground to the enemy. But as long as the survivals of a
premachine culture were still confidently robust, as long
as traditional morals still guided conduct, as long as a
religious sense of transcendental goals that outlasted the
lifetime of any single individual or nation kept operative, as long as a thousand habits and beliefs kept man's
funded values intact, the artist was not altogether a dis-
inherited or unemployed man. When the writer spoke
up in behalf of the human spirit, as Dickens did in *Hard
Times,* against the compulsive inhumanity of Gradgrind,

121

Bounderby, and M'Choakumchild, he could still address a responsive audience: men and women who had not yet fully submitted to the metaphysics and theology of the machine, people who still felt that man was the measure of all things, including the machine, and that God, that force and spirit both in the cosmos and in man himself which transcends the human, was the final goal of all true development. But these funded values, all these ancient foundations of man's very humanity have been shaken to their depths by the same general process that has undermined the arts. If only the external world and mechanical processes are real, then man himself has no status as a person: he is simply a thing, an accidental product of brute forces.

This false metaphysics was re-enforced and confirmed by the dismaying experience of the generation that fought World War I. Wholly unprepared for their ordeals, they found themselves, at the end, in a state of disillusionment, bitterness, and emptiness. No Romantic defiance, of the Byronic or Emersonian kind, was left in them. Feeling that the old theological and humanistic foundations had finally crumbled, the artist of that generation turned for support to the very ideas and institutions against which he had for so long been in blind, instinctive rebellion: at least the machine seemed to know its mind!

122

This acceptance of the machine was not altogether an unhealthy symptom, although it was certainly a somewhat belated response. For the weakness of the Romantic movement lay in the fact that it had looked backward, rather than forward, and it had rejected in any form the new instruments of thought and action that science had provided. Not that this mistake was a universal one. Early in the nineteenth century, in his *Defense of Poetry*, Shelley had suggested that one of the tasks of the artist in his day was to absorb the new knowledge of science and assimilate it to human needs, color it with human passions, transform it into the blood and bone of human nature. And that injunction had not been altogether unheeded by the poets of the nineteenth century: the belief in its possibility probably was one of the underlying bonds of sympathy between Tennyson, the author of *Locksley Hall*, and Whitman, the author of *Passage to India*. These poets felt, and felt rightly, that the new truths of science had a positive contribution to make to human life; so positive that one who respected them and took refuge in archaic feelings and images, was forfeiting a valuable part of his inheritance. There was, accordingly, something healthy and self-respecting, in the effort, from 1910 onward, to establish the artist as a willing participant in the new world of the machine;

and in the deliberate attempt to make use of new materials, new processes, new images, new rhythms.

This awakening to the values inherent in the machine was the positive side of the new movement in the arts during the last generation, a movement which, to reinforce its claims and bolster its self-confidence, revolted against the traditional forms of the past, against classic conceptions of human beauty, and proclaimed that the machine formed a self-enclosed and self-sufficient world of its own. In order to make sure of this advance, the artists who worked out its strategy blew up all communications lines, bridges, and ammunition dumps in the rear, and thus endangered their own position; but the movement was long overdue, and nothing I shall say by way of pointing out its limitations, should lead you to disparage or despise this very real achievement. It was important to realize, first with Louis Sullivan—or with Horatio Greenough long before him—that the machine, properly used, could be an agent of human order no less noble, indeed no less humane, within its own proper limits, than the traditional forms of handicraft. It was important to carry this intuition further, with Le Corbusier, and realize that the common products of mass production need not be nasty just because they were cheap; but might—as in a common drinking glass, a bentwood chair, a smoking pipe—have certain classic

124

qualities of form; so, too, a factory or a grain elevator, an airplane hangar or a steel bridge, might be as fine for their own purposes as a cathedral, a palace, or a stone bridge were for theirs. The error of these artists, an error pushed to its logical end in the polemics of Le Corbusier, did not consist in their thinking that the machine was important; their error lay in thinking that nothing else was important: particularly, in their tendency to despise every wish, every sentiment, every feeling, every purpose, except that which could be reduced to rational thought and mechanical order.

The machine, conceived as an organ subordinate to the human personality, is actually an instrument of liberation; but when mechanization takes command of man, diminishing every aspect of personality that does not fit into its rigidly defined ends, it leads to a progressive sterilization of the organic and the human; and this was in fact one of the most patent tendencies in the arts during the last thirty years. Up to this time, the passionate and personal animus of the artist had served as a counterpoise to mechanization. But after World War I, a one-sided accommodation to the machine became fashionable, first in the mind of the artist, then in every part of society. The other name for this process would be: The Displacement of Man. Human nature found itself empty-handed and unemployable and impotent; that diminution of the personality gave rise to mischief, and in time the mischief became malicious and even malignant: destructive and suicidal in its final effects.

By the end of this period, in advanced esthetic circles, all the great landmarks in art and thought were either defaced or reduced to mere dust and rubble; or at the very least, the shifting winds of doctrine had covered them over so completely with ideological sand that they remained almost invisible to the great mass of educated people. From the eighteenth century onward, indeed, one may say that life had been on the side of revolt in all the arts; and in that posture of affairs, it was easy to assume that the past, the traditional, the established, the historic, was always bad; and the future, the new, the revolutionary, was always good. This created a simple, if incredibly naïve, canon of judgment, one easy to apply and on the surface infallible: what was new was progressive and what was progressive was good. For those who held this view, the two constant aspects of all organic activity, stability and change, continuity and novelty, tradition and innovation, were regarded as hostile and irreconcilable forces. If one accepted change, novelty, and innovation, one rejected stability, continuity, and tradition; although without stability, change will lack direction and end, without

126

continuity, novelty may be only meaningless caprice, and without tradition, nothing that can properly be called a departure can be achieved. As a result of this convention of "automatic revolt," as one may call it, the human spirit was left without goals and purposes of its own; and the final result was a civilization as badly unbalanced on the side of the new, the mechanical, the antihuman, as the Middle Ages, in their decay, had been unbalanced on the side of the traditional, the obsolete, the effete, the unadventurously sane.

Difficult though it is to trace the process I have been attempting to interpret within the limits of a single lecture, I shall only be summing up an opinion on which a solid core of agreement has been reached by thinkers of the most diverse backgrounds, if I say that in our time we realize that the unqualified cult of mechanism leads to nihilism; and that nihilism, even if it were not equipped with the atom bomb and the H-bomb, would be capable of bringing to an end, not merely our civilization, but the human race itself. The critical moment when this change took place seems to be after World War I; though as with every social process there were various mutations and forerunners long before anything that could be called a movement had begun. One of the ideological harbingers of this change was the philosopher of history, Oswald Spengler, who in 1918 pro-

claimed that Western man was entering the winter of
his civilization, and that therefore he must abandon
lyric poetry for engineering, landscape painting and
symphonic music for business and administration, and
submit without murmur to the new mechanical barbarism that would govern the world through bloody and
brutal dictatorships. That philosophy gave overt expression to defeatist thoughts that had long been in the air.
In response to the conditions Spengler had called attention to, even if he misinterpreted them, various
manifestations of this withdrawal and shrinkage of the
human spirit took place in every department of art.

The same phenomena became as visible in painting
as in architecture. The new attitude was marked by an
overstress of technique and an indifference to values,
by an intensification of sensation—to the point of ex-
acerbation—and by a ruthless deflation of sentiment;
it was marked, above all, by a deliberate suppression of
emotion and feeling, or, as in the early novels of Aldous
Huxley, by a wry mockery of them. Confronted, for example, with love, the artist behaved like the irreverent
little boy who has never had such an adult experience:
he writes a dirty word on the wall and runs away,
because the experience is meaningless and valueless,
indeed altogether incomprehensible to him. This suppression of the organic, this sterilization of the emo-

tions, this desolate sense of man's emptiness and loneliness in an inhuman world, manifests itself, I say, in almost every department. In architecture it was accompanied by a special effort to give every building, no matter what its purpose, the neutrality, the machine-like quality, the bleak, colorless aspect of a factory building, housing machines whose products are never touched by human hands. Here the absence of color, texture, visible symbols of any kind, became the very test of esthetic sincerity. But what was this other than the change in the style of prose from the immense wealth and individual differences of nineteenth-century prose—from Emerson to Melville, from Carlyle to Arnold, from Newman to Ruskin—to the general acceptance of a neutral, colorless, nonrhythmical journalese, poor in images and lacking in musical quality, as the only possible medium of honest expression?

Those who conform to this canon have only one purpose, though they may never have formulated it in so many words: they seek to devaluate, to displace, to dehumanize—and so finally annihilate—the human personality. In despair of conquering the machine and humanizing the environment, because this would involve an act of self-regeneration which they are incapable of making, or even, it would seem, of conceiving, they turn upon man himself and deface his image. In summing up such a general attitude one naturally tends to use overemphatic blacks and whites, and to miss many important qualifications and gradations; but I think it is at least fairly just, and sufficiently discriminating, to say that the only choice before our civilization was either to accelerate all the mechanical processes that were bringing on catastrophe, or to change the whole purpose and plan of life by which we have lived. On those terms a large part of the art of revolt has not in fact been in favor of revolt or a fundamental change at all; it has rather been an act of conformity and surrender. What seemed a mere revolt against obsolete traditions was, when viewed more deeply, a determined attack upon the organic, the personal, the human aspects of life that can never be obsolete or old-fashioned.

If one puts aside all the purely meretricious manifestations of revolt in the arts—what was due to caprice, what was due to fashion, what was due to a mere desire to shock the once shockable middle classes—one will find at the core of the art of the last generation a serious preoccupation with an important though actually unformulated question: What would the world actually look like, how would man himself behave, if the axioms and premises of seventeenth-century science were wholly and exclusively true? That question will, I think, help us interpret the characteristic works of art produced by

130

many of the creative spirits of the last generation. It accounts for the absence of organic images and for the presence of mechanical phenomena or their symbolic equivalent. It accounts for a special respect for the geometrical or the abstract, as if the world were to be conceived, ultimately, solely by means of mathematical equations and formulas. It accounts for the cult of unintelligibility, which as it were, parrots the actual unintelligibility of most of the operations, within a laboratory or an automatic machine, to one who tries to understand what is taking place merely by means of the eye. Finally it accounts for the fact that the human personality, when it appears at all, is reduced either to its animal components, a bundle of reflexes and automatisms, or to an even remoter physical system—to a state in which the personality is the passive servant or victim of forces working outside it, and in which neither freedom nor responsibility, to say nothing of self-transcendence or self-perfection, is possible.

As with the physical sciences themselves, from their very origin, this movement carried with it both in painting and in literature a profound animus against the human. The most visible proof of that animus lies in what happened to the human body; for nothing that took place on the battlefield, in the bombed and obliterated city, or in the extermination camp, these last

131

thirty years, was more violent and dreadful than what happened on canvas, in the deliberate deformation, in the procrustean surgery, practiced upon the human body. The artist, mark you, was not recording something he actually saw: the works of art to which I am referring prophetically anticipate the catastrophes of life by a decade or two. In the early paintings of Chirico, against an urban landscape in which an ominous order has been purchased by the repression of every sign of life, the human body is represented by a stuffed, faceless dummy: the true symbol of a society that has accepted the regimentation of totalitarianism in any form. In the paintings of Picasso, the greatest draftsman of our time and possibly the greatest artist, every manner of deformation, accentuated by violent contrasts in color, was practiced upon the human image, once conceived as the very temple of divinity. Do not reproach the artist for making so clear the whole tendency of our civilization today; if such art was and is shocking, it is also medicinal, for, taken seriously, it would enable us to understand better the ultimate tendency of our whole civilization, as long as it continues to give power to machines that are almost human and to take away power, initiative, and autonomy, from human beings who thereby almost become machines. In a world denuded of all human values other than the exploitation of power, a world in which mechanisms have replaced organisms, only symbols of disintegration will do justice to the contents of life.

As long as the artist chains himself to the premises of seventeenth-century science, he must, to the extent that he is honest with himself and true to his intuitions, reveal the forces of destruction that are at large in the world. But we know now that both the premises and the conclusions of seventeenth-century science are manmade; and that the very displacement of man that has taken place in the last three centuries is itself an attempt to achieve order and law in a world whose subjective foundations had, indeed, crumbled, and needed to be rebuilt on deeper foundations.

Within science itself, the observer has come back into the picture, and every sensation, however austere, turns out to be a perception, that is, a subjective interpretation based upon symbols and signs, upon values and purposes, that man by his very being and history has brought into a universe that was otherwise without consciousness of meaning. Once more we understand that it is man's presence, with his high degree of sentience, his great range of feelings, his ample facilities for symbolic interpretation, that makes the difference. The real world, in other words, is the world that art and religion have always known: a world of cosmic perspectives and personal depths, a world of values and purposes, of forms and meanings, created by life for its own furtherance and self-transcendence. On the new premises, we look for patterns and wholes, in both time and space, and are never content with knowledge based upon disconnected parts, observed in discontinuous strips of time; and therefore instead of merely breaking down the complex into the simple, attempting to understand the aggregate by the parts, we see the further necessity of understanding the part by the whole, of judging the process by its consummation, of interpreting the universe itself in terms of its so-far-ultimate visible product: the human personality. On such scientific and philosophical foundations human life may again flourish, and the processes of integration may control those which otherwise are heading so rapidly toward disintegration—indeed toward an imminent and final catastrophe.

The situation for us today is quite different from the situation that produced, not merely seventeenth-century science, but the whole series of revolutions, political, industrial, social, esthetic, that followed along in its wake. It is not the dead past that threatens to choke life now, but rather the hyperactive present. Our danger springs not from a surfeit of traditional forms, many of which were effete and meaningless, as was true in both

134

the religion and art of the recent centuries. Our difficulty rises rather from a plethora of undigested and often indigestible novelty, produced by the revolutionary forces that are at work, without brake or impedance, in our society. The danger to the artist today is not that he will worship the past and copy the empty forms handed down from the past; the danger springs rather from an unwillingness to realize how poor and illiterate and misguided a generation is when it makes its own limited experience the sole criterion of the possibilities of life; for the experience of a single lifetime is not sufficient for measuring the dimensions and potentialities of human life as a whole. Man is wiser than men, and without the depths and perspectives of history, the future itself becomes merely a limited extrapolation of the present. The danger, finally, is not that man is the victim of hallucinations and untrammeled subjectivities that make it impossible for him to understand the nature of the external world; the danger is rather that his faith in the external and measurable will keep him from understanding experiences and values that are inaccessible to science, because they are subjective, private, and nonpredictable. We know at last, with redoubled conviction, something that the mechanical world picture sought to deny: that all that makes man specifically human is the result of his ability to project his own subjectivity, by means of dreams and words, symbols and forms of art and categories of thought, upon the groundwork of objective nature. If we try to castrate the organs of subjectivity, we reduce man himself to impotence: a creature, not a creator, the sport of random forces in a meaningless world.

The watchword for the coming era, therefore, is no longer revolution but integration and renewal. Yet in that process of integration all that was valuable in the revolutionary efforts of the last three centuries will be preserved and safeguarded by being incorporated into the dynamic pattern of the community and the personality, and directed to the renewal of life. This change, in the direction of integration, balance, organic wholeness, personalism, has been working under the surface during the last half-century, not least in the sciences themselves; and no generation has been altogether lacking in artists who have rejected the dehumanized ideology of our time. So, either by means of a private philosophy, like William Butler Yeats, or by association with a strictly traditional and conventional outlook, like T. S. Eliot, or by deeper metaphysical perceptions and affiliations, like Waldo Frank, these artists have sought to do more ample justice to human potentialities. Just as the generation of sculptors that so brutally assaulted the body still contained a Barlach and a Maillol, so the generation that responded too exclusively to the cacophonies and exacerbations and degradations of modern life still produced artists as deeply personal, as vigilantly healthy, and as humorously sane as Robert Frost, in poetry, and as John Marin in painting. Such artists are both survivals from the past and mutations toward a better future.

What seems to be happening among the younger artists today is that the sense of health and wholeness these older men have shown in their work, the respect for the specifically human, for the moral and the purposeful, no longer appears as an aberration but as the common mood of the new generation. They, too, realize that man can no longer be dismembered and live, that he cannot, under penalty of death, renounce his higher nature, reject the concepts of good and bad as meaningless, lose all habits of ethical discrimination and all sense of destination and a mission that transcends his mere biological survival. They realize that the human personality can no longer be looked upon as a mere intruder, an unwelcome visitor, in the natural world; but that, on the contrary, the human personality performs a central role in every operation, replacing automatism with purpose, modifying objectivity with tenderness and sympathy and life-sensitiveness, humanizing power with love. The dismembered man, he who had renounced his higher nature, will become knit together again like the dry bones Ezekiel saw in the Valley of Death. These artists realize that the task of the artist is to transpose life, in all its dimensions, into a significant and realizable whole; for in art alone, perhaps, does man fully live out his potentialities, in a medium he has created especially for his proper self-realization.

Since each generation, as I have just remarked, has always had artists who sought some sort of private integration, and sturdily resisted external forces of disruption when they proved too great to be controlled, belief in these new tendencies might turn out only a piece of wishful thinking, if one could find evidence of it only in the arts. But the fact is that we are dealing with a much wider process; and evidences of the new philosophy are at hand in every department of life, from childbirth and the nurture of children to medicine and education. Let us take one example close, very close, to home. The generation that was completely under the spell of mechanical principles and scientific depersonalization raised their young under a regime more inflexible, if that were possible, than the most Taylorized factory: a ghostly time clock presided over every moment of a child's day, punctuating with its inflexible discipline every biological function. Neither tears nor smiles, neither outrage nor affection on the part of the infant were supposed to hasten or delay any of these processes; and to make sure of that, the withdrawal of love by the parents, in any visible form, was demanded as a condition of success. By now most of the members of that generation know what the children themselves thought about this philosophy; they have revolted against this false science and this dehumanized regimen. Our more enlightened physicians have even discovered that the very processes of nutrition and repair require a loving atmosphere, if the calories and vitamins supplied are to prove effective nourishment. So that it turns out that many traditional methods of child care, even some of the traditional folklore that went with it, instead of being antiquated and useless, are more essential than most of the innovations that a crass, one-sided behaviorism introduced. This does not mean that we shall throw out the machine and the order it introduced; but it means that we shall put it in its place; that is, under the constant guidance, discipline, and control of man's highest functions, the functions of reason and love. If these changes can happen in the nursery, under pressure of an inner necessity, they can happen in the poet's study, the artist's studio, the playwright's theater, as the artists seek to project from within the forces that

139

may save humanity from its threatening degradations and catastrophes.

In no sense do the changes I have been trying to describe lead to a return to the past, considered as a fixed object and the source of unmodified standards. Though the sense of the organic I am describing can rediscover old values in Aristotle's concept of potentiality, it is not neo-Aristotelianism; though we understand more clearly the durable and constant elements in human life, the perpetual presentness of what theology calls the eternal, this is no mere resurrection of Platonism; and by the same token, what is vital in the reaction against the seventeenth-century world picture and the depersonalized world it has finally produced cannot be kept within the archaic confines of neo-Thomism. On the contrary, both in philosophy and in art, the change toward the organic and the personal will bring about a new synthesis, a synthesis no previous age was capable of formulating and expressing; for into this synthesis will go the fuller knowledge of the physical world we derive from Einstein, the deeper knowledge of the human psyche we derive from Freud, the greater sense of human mastery that we derive from our overprolific technology: in other words, the synthesis will transmute and ultimately utilize the very forces that now threaten us. We are moving, to refurbish Henry Adams's generalization, from twentieth-century multiplicity, with its specialisms, its divisions, its distortions, toward post-twentieth-century unity; and in our arts, as they receive these fresh currents of energy and hope, all of man's nature will be fully represented and utilized, not merely his instincts and reflexes and mechanical responses and physical needs, but all that makes him fully and eloquently human: above all, his capacities for understanding, sympathy, and love. The headline that the editors of the *Saturday Review* have used, "Even Good News Is News," might be applied to the human situation generally: Even the Good Life Is Life.

Let us confess it: the human situation is always desperate; and man's life is by nature precarious and mutable, delicately poised in an unstable equilibrium that a little excess of heat or a little shortage of water may completely overthrow. But today, all the normal mischances of living have been multiplied, a million-fold, by the potentialities for destruction, for an unthinking act of collective suicide, which man's very triumphs in science and invention have brought about. In this situation the artist has a special task and duty: the task of reminding men of the depth of their humanity and the promise of their creativity.

VII

IRRATIONAL ELEMENTS IN ART
AND POLITICS

Today we live in a world that, for the last thirty years, has been less and less governed by reason and love. The meaning of this nightmarish world, its whole intention and direction, was first grasped, I believe, by a group of modern artists who translated it into visible symbols, long before any but a few solitary observers like Henry Adams understood the facts of our time by historic and philosophic analysis. For this reason, one cannot understand the politics of our time, or the general state of our civilization, without interpreting the art of the last fifty years: for it is in painting and sculpture, sometimes decades before the event, that the facts of our life have been brought within an observable frame. At the same time, one cannot understand the latest developments in art, during the last decade particularly, without reference to the politics of our time, for the two are in a far closer relationship than either the politician or the artist has yet perceived.

Before I discuss the irrational elements in art and politics, it is important to make a fundamental discrimination, which applies to all the forces at work in our civilization. Those of us who came to modern art in our youth, with an almost crusading enthusiasm, often defended it against the pained criticisms of the traditionalists by saying that this new art, Post-Impressionism, Cubism, Futurism, Vorticism, or whatnot, was an "expression of our age"; and in that very fact we saw the proof of its validity and importance. But this judgment was formed on the basis of the great hope and confidence promoted by the previous Century of Progress, as it called itself, when we were sure that every new institution was better than the old, just because it came later, and we had not yet lived long enough to see that slavery, torture, the random extermination of civilian populations, might also be hailed, in the name of progress, as the wave of the future. Painfully we have at last learned that if art was an expression of our civilization, it might express these evils, in symbolic form, quite as readily as it expresses the positive and formative forces that had, in fact, a great contribution to make to man's development. We must distinguish, then, two processes at work in our civilization, one upbuilding, life-bestowing, life-regarding, the other de-building, destructive, life-betraying or life-denying, leading to ultimate extermina-

143

tion and annihilation. Modern art, departing from the traditional forms that had held sway since the Renaissance, responded to both sides of our existence; and the first step toward defining the irrational elements in art is to recognize and set apart those that arose, on the whole, out of the positive energies and vitalities in our civilization.

The radical transformation in art that dates from the death of Cézanne has accompanied and in part interpreted the radical transformations of space, time, and energy, in engineering and medicine, that have taken place within the last fifty years. No close correspondence between the symbols of art and the conceptions of science should be looked for: indeed the attempt to justify the appearance of a few erratic spots on a modern canvas by reference to a photographic plate dealing with the path of an atomic particle, is specious, not to say pathetic, for if true it would reduce the mission of the modern painter to mere illustration. If one recalls Renaissance painting, which was contemporary with the great age of exploration, one is astonished to find so few images of the new world that disclosed itself to the traveler and the adventurer: but if one looks closer, both the sea captain and the painter employed the same method of locating objects in space, by drawing fixed

144

co-ordinates, by means of which the ship's course or the object's boundaries could be accurately plotted.

So with modern art during the last half century: by its very detachment from the Renaissance world of ordered objects, viewed from a fixed position in space, it has disclosed the new multidimensional world revealed by science and carried into our daily life by invention. This is a world in which fixed relations between objects are altered by speed, and in which both rapid travel and long-distance communications superimpose upon the environment in which we familiarly operate, one or more other vivid environments that warp the photographic image. Marcel Duchamp's famous "Nude Descending a Staircase" was a startlingly realistic anticipation of the results of the dissection of motion by the stroboscopic camera, as disclosed a few decades later by Gjon Mili. So, too, though the Renaissance painter, to perfect his mastery of surface form and volume, took the lead in the dissection of the human body, it is only in our time, with the advance of scientific analysis, and the revelations of the X-ray, that the subcutaneous reality of organs, tissues, and cells has become part of our daily consciousness.

For us, today, reality no longer can be represented fully by surface images: the invisible is as real, as present, as operative as that which is open to our immediate

145

gaze. I would not say that this multidimensional world has often been adequately represented or symbolized in any public form, except perhaps in the terrifying abstraction of three-dimensional chess; still less that many artists have succeeded in translating it into intelligible and orderly symbols of art; but the sculptures of the Constructivists, particularly of Naum Gabo, come close to revealing and interpreting the new world of space, time, energy, motion, and to constructing equivalent forms that captivate the spirit. On the whole this art has been a healthy influence; and the same can be said, with certain reservations, for the effort, led by the Cubists more than a generation ago, to do justice to machines and machine forms as objects of perception. This was a task in which photographers, beginning with Stieglitz, painters beginning with Duchamp-Villon and Léger, sculptors beginning with Brancusi, and architects, beginning afresh with Le Corbusier, have united to acclimate the mind and spirit of man to the new machine-conditioned, machine-made world that he was creating. By contemplating these new forms, by extracting from them new values, quickened sensuous perceptions, often perceptions of great fineness and delicacy, as in the paintings of Loren MacIver, modern man made himself at home in the very world from which the antiseptic, dehumanized procedures of science had excluded him. That too

146

was a gain in values: likewise a gain in spiritual balance, provided the machine was not conceived as a demiurge that ruled all other human needs.

One more aspect of modern art, on the positive and affirmative side, must be mentioned—though it is an ambivalent contribution and from the first showed disturbing openness to the forces of disintegration. This has to do with the multidimensional nature of the human personality, with all the interrelations that exist between the inner and the outer, from the autonomic nervous system and the preconscious processes to the subtlest manifestations of thought and feeling: with all the layers of self from the id to the superego. Thanks to Sigmund Freud, our age has rediscovered and re-established the inner world: the world of fantasy and dreams, that spontaneous fountain of free creativity, in which nothing is probable because everything is possible, a world in which the demonic and angelic are forever at war. A generation ago, the Expressionists and the Surrealists began to interpret this world for us, often retaining some of its most endearing qualities; its humor, as in the delicate fantasies of Klee and Chagall, in the droll contraptions of Pierre Roy, even occasionally in the deliberately paranoid art of Dali, as in the painting of the half-melted watches depending limply from a tree. Esthetically, these images were often fragmentary: sym-

147

bolically they existed in a self-enclosed void. But many of the Surrealists, whose work seems to rise out of the blackest depths of the unconscious, also turned out to be much closer to the increasingly grim realities of the outer world.

I keenly recall my own premonitory uneasiness at seeing the blasted landscapes and dismantled factories in Lurçat's paintings of the early thirties: they prepared one for the destruction of the coming war, as the mutilated human forms that appeared in Surrealist art prepared one for the nauseating horrors of Hitler's extermination camps. The exacerbating sensations, the emotional violence, the actual tortures and butcheries, of the period of victorious Fascism—the period dominated by Hitler and Stalin—could be interpreted only in distorted forms and sadistic images, forms close to the productions of madness, in a picture like Picasso's famous Guernica mural. The human content of those pictures was sometimes so unbearable that they raised the question as to whether the artist himself was merely portraying the evil and madness of our age, or actually, by his very images, participating in it and extending its influence—just as our comic books and our gangster motion pictures and radio plays actually do on the lowest everyday level.

At the first try many of these manifestations of modern art might seem as difficult for a layman to interpret as the latest equation of nuclear physics. But in time the more positive productions, associated with the more formative processes in our civilization, became individually more intelligible, though anything like a synthesis between the various aspects of life and reality that have been symbolized in art during the last fifty years has so far proved unattainable: indeed, just the opposite has happened, because with the further development of painting, particularly in America, the split between the integrating and the disintegrating tendencies has become deeper. That split has become as deep, in fact, as the difference between the deeply human life-furthering purposes of UNRRA and the Marshall Plan (in its original form) and the antihuman and life-threatening purposes associated all over the world—and above all in our own country—with the development of agents of atomic and bacterial extermination.

One part of our art has responded to the formative and rational elements in our civilization and has sought to interpret and translate them: the other part has responded to, has recorded, has intensified the horror and misery and madness of our age, with its code of unrestricted violence and its scientifically contrived technics of demoralization, disintegration, and extermination. As one looks back over the art of the last forty years, these two facts are increasingly plain, and the ways which seemed to run parallel at first have parted further and further. Plainly, the narrow path, the path of discipline, order, rationality, discrimination, the path of mature and loving emotional development, fruitful and creative in every occasion it embraces, has become ever narrower, and the effort to follow its upward course has become lonelier and lonelier. Those artists who are committed to this way have fallen out of fashion; and sometimes, for lack of response, have ceased actively to create. While, on the other hand, the broad path, the path that leads to destruction—to the corruption of the human, to the denial of love, to systematized disorder, to non-communication and non-intercourse at any level—has become wider and wider. So it is in art; so it is in politics. The glorification of brutality characterizes all the arts today: both highbrow and lowbrow have become connoisseurs of violence. The enemies of the human race are no longer isolated tyrants, like Hitler and Stalin: in the very act of opposing their programs of revolutionary enslavement by the same means these dictators employed, we ourselves have increasingly taken on their inhuman or irrational characteristics.

As if the cult of violence were not a sufficient threat to our rationality, indeed to our very humanity, the painting of our time discloses still another danger: the surrender to the accidental and the denial of the possibility of coherence and intelligibility: what one might call the devaluation of all values and the emptying out of all meanings. This ultimate expression of the meaningless began in an almost innocent, because still humorous, form, at the end of World War I, in the cult of Dadaism: an irreverent commentary on the inflated platitudes of politicians. But by now the cult of the meaningless is a grimly humorless one: the negative responses that its empty splotches and scrawls at first provoke in a perceptive mind will be met, on the part of the devotees, with a fanatic gleam of reproach. Cracks, erosions, smudges, denials of all order or intelligibility, with not even as much capacity for evocative association as a Rorschach ink blot—this is the ultimate form and content of the fashionable art of the last decade. To gaze piously into this ultimate emptiness has become the last word in art appreciation today. The artists who produce these paintings, or the sculptures that correspond to them, are often people of serious talent: sometimes their early work discloses the fact that they were people of original ability, perfectly able as far as technical command of the means goes, to express whatever human thought or feeling the artist of any age might express. But now all their talent, all their energy, is concentrated on only one end: a retreat, not only from the surface world of visible buildings and bodies, but a retreat from any kind of symbol that could, by its very organization, be interpreted as having a connection with organized form: a retreat into the formless, the lifeless, the disorganized, the dehumanized: the world of nonsignificance, as close as possible to blank nonexistence.

In these final images the modern artists who seem, however patiently we behold them, to say nothing to us, are in fact saying a great deal. Paintings that we must, in all critical honesty, reject as esthetic expressions, we must yet accept as despairing confessions of the soul, or as savage political commentary on our present condition arising from the depths of the unconscious. For there is one special quality in these paintings that lowers their standing as works of art: they are too factual, too realistic, they are too faithful reflections of the world we actually live in, the world we are so energetically preparing to suffer death in. These symbols of nothingness, true revelations of our purposeless mechanisms and our mechanized purposes, this constant fixation on what is violent, dehumanized, infernal—all this is not pure esthetic invention, the work of men who have no contacts with the life around them. Just the contrary: their ultimate negation of form and meaning should remind us of the goal of all our irrational plans and mechanisms. What they say should awaken us as no fuller and saner images might. These men, these paintings, these symbols have a terrible message to communicate: their visual nihilism is truer to reality than all the conventional paintings that assure us so smoothly that our familiar world is still there—and will always be there.

Let us not reproach the artist for telling us this message, which we have not the sensitivity to record or the courage to tell to ourselves: the message that the future, on the terms that it presents itself to us now, has become formless, valueless, meaningless: that in this irrational age, governed by absolute violence and pathological hate, our whole country, our whole civilization, might vanish from the face of the earth as completely as images of any sort have vanished from these pictures: as dismayingly as that little isle in the Pacific vanished from the surface of the ocean under the explosion of the hydrogen bomb. This is the new apocalypse, haunted by more terrible specters than the traditional Four Horsemen, as they appeared to the innocent eyes of John of Patmos— a revelation that promises neither a new heaven nor a new earth but an end that would nullify and make meaningless the whole long process of human history. Let the painters who have faced this ultimate nothingness, who have found a symbol for it, be understood if not honored: what they tell us is what we are all hiding from ourselves.

We are living in a society whose present character and condition were first prophetically disclosed in two American tales, that of Hawthorne's *Ethan Brand* and that of Herman Melville's *Moby Dick*. Ethan Brand, the lime burner, the prototype of the dehumanized technician, by seeking knowledge and power alone cuts himself off by degrees from the magnetic chain of humanity: in the end he incinerates himself in his own furnace. As for Melville's epic, his Captain Ahab, who rejects the claims of both divine and human love, finally grapples with his consecrated enemy, the White Whale, only to bring himself and his ship to utter destruction—though for an instant, before the pursuit has reached its climax, he says to himself in one last flash of lucidity: "All my means are sane; my motives and object, mad."

Unfortunately for us today the means have now become as irrational as our purposes; for in the very act of piling up weapons of extermination our leaders constantly assure us, with a laudable anxiety that alas! reveals their inner confusion, not only that there can be no victory, but that the employment of these instruments might wipe out the human race, or even destroy all life on the planet. That contradiction between our totali-

tarian military instruments and our democratic political
ends gives the final measure of the irrationality of our
time. Our works of love have marvelously succeeded:
witness the rebuilding of Europe under the Marshall
Plan. But our works of power have miserably failed.
Most of the means we have taken to ensure military victory, during the last ten years, have so far led to defeat.
The measures we have adopted for national security
have enormously magnified every danger and enslaved
us to our fears: the measures we have taken to detect
traitorous accomplices of the Russian state have subverted the American Constitution more effectively than
thirty years of Communist espionage and plotting: the
measures we have taken to promote the physical sciences
rapidly have led to the stultification of that great scientific tradition of intercommunication, which alone made
possible the fission of the atom. In the name of freedom
we are rapidly creating a police state; and in the name
of democracy we have succumbed, not to creeping socialism but to galloping Fascism, in which official scan-
dal sheets spotted with unsorted lies, fabrications, and
distortions, have been used in an attempt to destroy
overnight the reputation and political effectiveness of
honorable, patriotic men, like Bishop Oxnam. While
our jet planes can girdle the earth at a faster rate than
sound, freedom of travel and communication among

scholars and men of science is now curtailed, not only in Russia but in the United States, on grounds as capricious and nonsensical as the whole legal process that Kafka described in his prophetic novel, *The Trial*.

Yes: *The Trial* is the great symbol of this period of irrational politics. Each one of us, as in Kafka's novel, is likely to have his life disposed of—individually and collectively—by irresponsible powers, powers insidiously automatic, impervious to rational direction, deaf to human pleas and petitions; powers he is never allowed to confront, powers he is never able to challenge, powers that operate in the dark under remote compulsions that have no rational basis and no valid human purpose. In such a state of society, which I analyzed with some fullness in *The Conduct of Life,* the higher functions of the human spirit become paralyzed, and authority passes to the lower functions, to automatisms and reflexes, to primitive urges that have not undergone rational scrutiny and that have not been directed toward high and humane goals. When this happens, we do not return to a merely animal level: we return to a plane far below that, at which point we may lose even the animal's aptitude for challenge, resistance, insurgence: in short, for striking back.

Too many of us have already descended to the level of the docile robot, manipulated by remote control. But note this: when human beings are cut off from a purposeful and meaningful life, they not merely lose the animal capacity for self-preservation, but even the very will to live. This propensity to self-destruction is the nemesis of irrationality; but unfortunately, with the powers that we now command, before we destroy our enemy and ourselves, we may also destroy the whole fabric of mankind's life. Lord Acton's oft-repeated dictum on the pathology of power, that "Power corrupts and absolute power corrupts absolutely," is now undergoing its final demonstration. We are living in an age when finite human beings, subject to sin and error, beings of plainly limited intellectual capacities, open to erratic promptings, have assumed control of energies of cosmic dimensions. That dangerous fact has been made infinitely more dangerous by the wall of secrecy that has been erected around these powers, and by the atmosphere of fear, suspicion, isolation, noncommunication that the very nature of these destructive weapons and instruments has helped to produce. As a result, issues that concern humanity as a whole have been treated as if they were of purely national concern; plans and policies that should have been subject to open discussion and earnest moral debate have been made in closed chambers without benefit of public reflection by men with minds even more tightly shut than the doors that guarded them. Nowhere has the democratic process, indeed the bare protections of constitutional government, been more consistently flouted than in the field of preparation for total genocide. Nowhere have moral judgments been more completely paralyzed than in the very area where moral judgments alone could preserve our humanity.

There is indeed one grave flaw in all these irrational preparations: they cannot afford the risk of open public discussion, of intelligent reassessment of the means to be used and the ends to be achieved, of rigorous and realistic moral judgment. Such judgment not only concerns itself with the principle of doing reverence to all life, but it understands that there are moral norms—natural laws if not divine commands—that no self-respecting person, *yes, and no self-respecting nation,* can afford to violate merely to preserve their own existence.

Because this flaw is a serious one, the general conspiracy of silence that now prevails must be fortified by the invention of a new heresy and a new crime: a crime more serious than that of sympathizing with Communism or of engaging in treasonable activities on behalf of Soviet Russia. The crime I refer to—forgive me for countenancing this heresy—is the crime of being human. Who are the marked men and women among us today? Who are the ultimate security risks? They are the people who still retain and still cherish all their human attributes; people who are trusting, tenderhearted, responsive, co-operative, curious, intelligent, humorous, capable of human sympathy and love. People who read widely and think critically, who are not afraid to exchange opinions with those they differ from, who trust their neighbors and are magnanimous to their enemies, who believe in freedom for others as well as for themselves; people who are fully committed to democracy, who are ready to challenge arbitrary authority, and rise as Walt Whitman commanded "against the never-ending audacity of elected persons." Such people, the very salt of American democracy, hold a hand uplifted over irrationality, if not over fate; and fortunately, as long as they exist, not by the thousands, but by the tens of millions, there is still a prospect of recovering from the state of collective paranoia, of pathological suspicion and isolation, into which our country has so swiftly fallen.

The leaven of Christianity is still at work among these sweetly sane people, and the lessons of the New Testament, so easy to disregard in happier times, have come home to them as perhaps the ultimate word in practical statesmanship, if we are not to resign ourselves prematurely to mankind's annihilation through the misuse of the very forces man's intellect has brought to light. There will be no lifting of the catastrophic threat that hangs over mankind, making blank and valueless all activities that conserve the past and mold the future, until we recover as a nation the capacity to be human again. The preliminary step toward justice and peace, toward trustful human intercourse between peoples, is the capacity to feel love in our hearts, and to bestow love even on our enemies, in the hope of reawakening their own humanness, their own potential capacity for love. It is easy, as Henry James, Sr., once remarked, to love those who love us, or who are in themselves lovable. But true love demands something more than that: it requires that we do good to them that hate us and use us despitefully; for only such love can transcend our easy, self-justifying repulsions and remove, from our enemy's heart, his abiding fear of our own hateful intentions. Anything that can be called statesmanship today rests on the practice of love, of a love that is capable of self-abnegation and self-sacrifice, of a humility and patience as deep as Lincoln expressed in his Second Inaugural Address. By the same token, any policy that rests on the delusions of grandeur and pride in possession of absolute power must be as self-defeating, indeed as suicidal, as is the degraded mental state of which it is, in fact, the clinical expression.

Need we carry the political or esthetic analysis any

further? The theme of this paper is not, it goes without saying, open to any laboratory demonstration. All I could hope to do was to indicate a possible connection between the disturbing symbols of fashionable modern art, so empty, so valueless and meaningless, so chaotic and random, and the deeply irrational quality taken on by political life today, in which absolute power has become another name for impotence, in which security becomes more terrifyingly absent with every new physical instrument invented to produce it, in which the final destination of our whole civilization could be represented only by such a form as unorganized and meaningless particles floating at random about an otherwise vacant canvas.

In both art and politics we have reached the last blank wall of meaninglessness: the complete negation of all human values and purposes. That is the ABC lesson of the ABC war—the seemingly innocent classification that has been given to atomic, biological, and chemical genocide. The only intelligible fact that post-Abstract painting discloses is that life has become purposeless. The only idea that is conveyed by its lack of form and design is that the next step—and the last one—is chaos: the chaos of a final wasteland in which all order and design derived from life have returned to aimless dust and rubble. In bringing these new facts and these new symbols together, I have, I hope, at least opened the way for a clearer insight into the human problems of our time: problems that transcend art and science and politics. The corrupt purposes that we passively participate in, the immoral acts we have accepted in the name of expediency or practicality or even of financial economy, the irrational compulsions that we have bowed to with the respect we owe only to reason—all these things are not fixed and fated. We need not submit to these dehumanized processes and these life-negating mechanisms. To be human is to understand, to evaluate, to choose, to accept responsibility. As Robinson Jeffers once wrote, corruption never was compulsory, and the existentialist, Sartre, has more recently made the same observation.

We have *made* ourselves into the creatures we have, so deplorably, become. Let us look at that new image in the national mirror, and be properly horrified and frightened by it. *Is this America?* Is this walled-in enclosure we have locked ourselves into a home or an asylum? Let us look into the eyes of our foreign neighbors, at our friends in other parts of the world, and understand why they are so deeply shocked by what they see. Once we have seen ourselves, we need not maintain a discreet silence about our condition—as I have tried, in the course of this paper, modestly to demonstrate. We have still another choice open: the choice of renewing our integrity, our sanity, our humanity.

And this brings me, finally, back to the artist, whose last message I have tried to interpret. If he is not to betray his art as well as his humanity, he must not think that nausea and vomit are the ultimate realities of our time. Those obscenities are indeed a part of the actual world we are conditioned to; but they do not belong to the potential world of the creator and transvaluer, who brings forth out of his own depths new forms and values that point to new destinations. The artist, too, has the responsibility to be sane, the duty to be whole and balanced, the obligation to overcome or transform the demonic and to release the more human and divine elements in his own soul: in short, the artist has the task of nourishing and developing every intuition of love and of finding images through which they become visible. If all he can say in his pictures is, "This is the end"— let it be the end and let him say no more about it. Let him be silent until he has recovered the capacity to conjure up once more, however timidly at first, a world of fine perceptions and rich feeling, of values that sustain life and coherent forms that re-enforce the sense of human mastery.

No one has fully taken in all the new dimensions of our world; no one effectively commands all the forces that are now at humanity's disposal. But we know that mankind today, thanks to the pooling of reserves and treasures from every culture and historic epoch, including our own, is in possession of energies, vitalities, humanities, and divinities now only feebly and fitfully used, which are capable of redeeming our civilization. Catastrophe is perhaps nearer to us than salvation, as a war of unrestricted extermination is perhaps nearer to us than the foundation of universal peace, based on justice and loving co-operation: but the destructive nightmare, in whose grip mankind is now so helplessly tossing and turning, is no more real than the benign dream.

We need the help of the artist to rally, by his example and effective demonstration, the forces of life, the passionate commitments of love, to recall to us all the qualities we have violated this last century in the untrammeled pursuit of power. Henry Adams's "Prayer to the Virgin," as the only possible answer to those cosmic forces he—almost alone—had the insight to anticipate and foretell, must be rewritten and repainted in a thousand expressive ways. Every word of the final invocation of the last few stanzas has meaning for us today. And first of all: "Help [us] to see," for it is our unseeingness that has permitted us to stumble so close to the edge of the abyss. "Help us to know," for the withholding of knowledge and the reluctance to draw conclusions from the knowledge we do possess, add willful ignorance to willful blindness. But above all we must recover that which we have lost through the very techniques of scientific knowledge and invention: the power to feel, which is at the basis of all truly human relationships, for once sympathy, pity, and love are withdrawn, intelligence will likewise fail us, and we shall treat other men as if they were mere things or objects. Let us remember, then, those final words of Henry Adams's invocation to the Virgin: "Help us to *feel*, not with our insect sense, with yours that felt all life alive in you: infinite heart beating at your expense, infinite passion, breathing the breath you drew." Yes: help us to *feel*. Our numbness is our death. Whatever our immediate fate may be, as individuals or as a nation, we must, as a condition of survival, recover our humanity again: the capacity for rational conduct, free from compulsive fears and pathological hatreds: the capacity for love and confidence and co-operation, for humorous self-criticism and disarming humility, in our dealings with each other, and in our dealings with the rest of the human race, including, it goes without saying, our enemies. Even should we meet disaster or death through the attempt to replace the politics of dehumanized and absolute power by the politics of love, that defeat would only be a temporary one. For the God in us would remain alive—to quicken the spirit of those that follow us.

VIII

THE UPRISING OF CALIBAN

We have the misfortune to live under the sign of Caliban. Hate, fear, suspicion, violence have become almost endemic. In America, abnormality is fast becoming our norm: automatism our overruling providence: irrationality itself the criterion of reason. Fantasies of wholesale extermination and annihilation no longer fill only the minds of certified paranoiacs: their studious translation into the practical devices of atomic, biological, and chemical warfare has dominated the activities of leaders in science and government for more than a decade.

These practical preoccupations, so quietly pursued, have given a deceptive air of sanity to projects that match the hallucinations of more obvious victims of mental disease, confined to hospitals for the incurably insane. At lower levels, the same methodical irrationality prevails under the sober guise of law, order, national security. Though in every period disintegrating forces tend to break through the crust of orderly life, in our age they have broken through at so many points that

166

they have formed a second crust: indeed, they have spread so widely and hardened so solidly that they threaten to suppress every benign manifestation of life.

For the sake of brevity, and for reasons that will become plainer as I go on, I propose to personify the demoralizing forces of modern barbarism by the figure of Caliban. That fawning brute, that gibbering fool, that snarling animal, as Shakespeare pictured him in *The Tempest,* may well stand as image of the lower powers of man—of nature untouched by nurture, to use Shakespeare's own terms—against whose uprising and domination no person, no civilization, is ever entirely safe.

In an effort to curb this creature, earlier societies had made him a prisoner and thrust him into a dungeon, treating him with a savageness that disclosed the proper fear that the ever-seductive temptation to relapse into brutishness provokes in the human breast. To make reparation for that harsh attitude, our more humanitarian age, prompted by a complacent naturalism and a misapplied egalitarianism, put Caliban on the same level as Prospero, and accorded him an equal degree of power and authority. In repayment for this kindness, Caliban now refuses to acknowledge that there is any higher power than his own: indeed, higher and lower are meaningless terms to him, along with good and bad, creative and destructive; but insofar as his behavior implies a recognition of difference, he is on the side of the destroyer. As a result, the problem of our time, the problem that holds a key to every other issue, is to bring Caliban back once more under the control of Prospero.

In contrast to Caliban, Prospero is the incarnation of man's higher powers. His is the discerning intelligence that foresees and anticipates, in a state of constant alertness against blind habit and meaningless automatism. His is the sensitive morality that weighs and evaluates, restrains and directs human conduct; his is the brooding imagination that, by means of art and love, fashions a fresh form for man's every activity, a more human mask for the face and character of man, and a higher destiny for his life.

To Prospero, finally, belongs the religious insight that seeks to unite the limited purposes of man with cosmic processes that outlast his brief existence; and through Prospero's very ability to interpret these processes, he takes over nature's responsibilities and turns them more consciously into the path of development and perfection. If Caliban is brute vitality and energy, undirected and self-destructive, Prospero is potentiality and purpose, value and meaning, power molded by form, providentially directed to the service of man's present life and toward the development of a greater life that shall transcend its limitations.

Caliban is the symbol of the primitive unconscious forces in man which, when neither controlled by morals nor expressed by art, offer a greater threat to reason and love than their more obvious enemies. My figures are as simple, indeed as old-fashioned, as that; and though they may mean more than Shakespeare himself intended, they can be translated, without too great distortion, into the terms of modern analytical psychology. If your Shakespeare fails you, Dr. Sigmund Freud will stand you in stead: for Caliban, read the id, the primitive underworld self, and for Prospero the superego, even though I shall define that superego in more generous terms than Freud used. If, again, you prefer the symbols of theology, you will be equally near my meaning if you identify Caliban with the demonic and Prospero with the divine.

Now those of you who have grown up during the past forty years may, for lack of any other kind of experience, believe that the inordinate violence and irrationality of our times have always characterized our civilization. Most of you cannot remember, as I do, the look of incredulous horror on everyone's face when they read the morning papers on a May day some thirty-nine years ago, and found that the steamer *Lusitania*, a ship loaded with a few hundred passengers, had been sunk without warning by a German submarine. The shock

169

of that event went far deeper than the first Fascist bombing of civilians in Madrid during the Franco uprising against the constitutional Spanish republic; and that, in turn, was greater than the horror evoked by the wiping out by the Nazis of thirty thousand Dutch civilians in the center of Rotterdam. Again, that event seemed more dreadful, at least to Americans, than our own extermination of one hundred thousand civilians (along with fifty thousand soldiers) in Hiroshima, by our dropping of the first atomic bomb in 1945.

Note that in thirty brief years, violence and slaughter had increased at geometric ratio, while the human reaction to it had altered inversely. Yet the obnoxious principle in all these cases—the ruthless killing of helpless noncombatants under the guise of military necessity—remained the same. Mankind's long sustained effort to limit the area of slaughter and rapine even in warfare has been halted in our own age: indeed, its direction has been reversed. Modern war, pursued to its logical end, means not the defeat of the enemy but his total extermination: not the resolution of the conflict but the liquidation of the opposition. This is the characteristic Caliban note of our time: one that is coming more and more to dominate both domestic and foreign politics.

The import of this fact apparently has not penetrated the armor of habit that protects sensitive persons: even professed pacifists fail to make any distinction between the limited violence of warfare, brutal though that is, and the unlimited violence of mass extermination. Few of you, perhaps, can remember the time when it was taken for granted that the poisoning of the enemy's water supply, for the purpose of embarrassing his army, was no longer permissible, indeed no longer thinkable, as an act of war. In those days our current preparations for wholesale extermination—extermination by poisoning water and atmosphere, by utilizing nerve gases and lethal bacteria lest any vestige of life by chance escape the hydrogen bombs—would have been regarded, even by coarse, unfeeling people, as the proposals, not of men, but of demented brutes. Such measures violate the principle that Immanuel Kant laid down in his essay *On the Nature of Peace:* "Confidence in the principles of an enemy must remain even during war, otherwise peace could never be concluded." When hostilities "degenerate into a war of extermination" the means befoul every justifiable human end.

One final story, trivial but no less significant, will give the measure of the change in the moral climate that began in 1914. Early in World War I, when German Zeppelins had begun to raid London by night, Bernard Shaw wrote to the *Times* of London to suggest that the London County Council build air-raid shelters for their school children, in anticipation of Germany's widening the method of attack. The editors of the *Times* were so indignant over Shaw's suggestion that they barely consented to print the letter; and in an editorial they reproved Shaw for being so irresponsible as to hint even in jest that a civilized government, like that of Germany, would ever stoop so low as to bomb civilians from the air. There was no need for Shaw to defend himself against that reproof: the Germans themselves supplied the answer.

I cite these facts, a handful from among a score I could draw on, to show that the violence and irrationality to which we have become calloused differ both in kind and in amount from that which one discovers in happier periods of history. Even if a growing part of the population has made Caliban their god, we have no reason to think that the kingdom and power have always been his. What, indeed, is the history of the last five thousand years of civilization, but the continued attempt, often halted, sometimes set back, but never permanently defeated, to restrict the powers of Caliban and to elevate those of Prospero?

But if we must not make the error of thinking that violence and irrationality, in their present quantities, are normal, we must equally be on guard against another illusion, more flattering to our egos, more soothing to our patriotic pride: the notion that these moments of disintegration are peculiar to peoples who, like the Germans, the Russians, or the Japanese, have long been subjected to a repressive, authoritarian government, and have not been moralized, as we have been, by the more reasonable and co-operative practices of democracy. That illusion perhaps seemed plausible in the thirties, when the contrasts between the practices of American democracy and totalitarian absolutism were more sharp than (to our shame) they now are. During that decade the democratic forces in our country had proved their capacity to meet any emergency under the Constitution, even the most paralyzing of economic depressions, without forfeiting liberty or even impairing the rights of property, despite the confident proselytism and active intervention of both communism and Fascism. But by now we must realize that we have no natural immunity against either spontaneous or organized Calibanism. We have still some distance to go before we sink to the Russian level of political intimidation and repression; but in relation to our own conceptions of human decency and freedom, we have already sunk far too low.

Too easily, indeed, during the past decade, we have attempted to cover up our own uneasiness by redoubling our outrage over the conduct of our enemies: the familiar Freudian device of the transferred reproach. We continue to be indignant over the Iron Curtain that the Communist-dominated countries have lowered, to prevent easy travel and spontaneous social intercourse; but we forget that even under the administration of President Truman, the State Department and the Congress had erected an Iron Curtain of our own, somewhat more open-meshed, but just as arbitrary in its prohibitions. Restrictions upon free movement and social intercourse, normal, indeed indispensable, in wartime, have hardened into daily routine: people who have no criminal record and no official secrets have been confined to this country by administrative act—the withholding of a passport—as if it were a prison; and candidates for high public office are now subjected to the gratuitous humiliation of security investigations, as if the unedited dossiers of our secret police, filled with anonymous scurrilities, were a reputable means of bolstering public confidence in a loyalty that should, in a normal society, not ridden by pathological suspicion and fear, be taken for granted. If the fathers of our country had been as frenetically alarmed by Benedict Arnold's treason, and loyalism generally, as our present-day governments have been by the threat of Communist subversion, they would have anticipated the French Revolution by instituting a Reign of Terror in the name of Public Safety, and thrown our young republic behind the bars of a Police

State. Instead, they deliberately extended the protection of the Bill of Rights to all suspected criminals, even traitors.

Next to disregarding entirely the threat of Caliban to our civilization, the worst folly would be to identify him solely with Nazism or totalitarian communism, and to disregard the many evil features and gestures that can already be detected in our own country.

Even if by some providential exhibition of prudence and forbearance we were insured against any major outbreak of international genocide for the next century, that is no guarantee that the forces of Caliban, if otherwise unchecked, might not be dominant at the end of that time. Our children might indeed escape wholesale incineration; and yet find that what had begun as a tentative cold war against Soviet Russia had turned into a permanent cold war, a deepfreeze war, against every human faculty that did not lend itself to mechanical standardization or governmental control: a war against all those people, native or foreign, who differed in thought or attitude from our self-imposed totalitarian orthodoxy. In the act of closing ranks to face the worst we might, in fact, produce the worst.

George Orwell's nightmare world of 1984 is already uncomfortably near. The verbal rewriting of American history, in close imitation of the Russian precedent, has

175

already begun; and if Presidents Truman and Roosevelt
have been publicly referred to as traitors or the accomplices of traitors, it will not be long, if this state of
mind solidifies, before Woodrow Wilson and Thomas
Jefferson will be included in the same category. Whitman, Melville, Thoreau, and Emerson, to say nothing of
Lowell and Howells, will vanish from our libraries for
the same reason, in an effort to convert the freedom that
characterized our past into the inquisitorial authori-
tarianism that threatens our present and may doom our
future.

So much for the outward signs of Caliban. But if we
would be wrong to impute all these symptoms to our
present national enemies alone, we would be equally
wrong if we imagined that a few malign or honestly mis-
taken men, in official positions, could by themselves
bring about this general lowering of public morality,
or that a mere weapon of destruction could by itself
produce the other characteristic symptoms of this self-
induced illness—baseless suspicion, hostility, random
violence, non-cooperation, and non-communication. In
diagnosing the collective psychosis that now threatens to
break out on an even wider scale, we must not make the
mistake, which medicine once made with regard to disease, of attempting to isolate only the individual germ
and to locate the particular areas of infection. That

kind of analysis is important; but it is equally necessary to understand the general state of the whole organism and to identify the factors that have lowered
its immunity. If we are forthright in our analysis, we
shall have to admit, I believe, that inroads Caliban has
already made indicate more fundamental weaknesses in
our philosophy and faith. Perceptive observers, like
Delacroix the painter and Burckhardt the historian, had
ominous premonitions of the coming barbarism a full
century ago. For this reason, an adequate diagnosis may
keep us from spending too much time dealing with
mere symptoms: it should rather be general enough to
open the way for a more radical correction of our whole
regimen.

Our delay in understanding the processes of disintegration at work in our time has, perhaps, been due
to the fact that, both in Soviet Russia and in the United
States, Caliban has crept into our homes, not as a
marauding beast, but in the guise of a friend, bringing
special gifts. In Russia he promised justice and equality, the removal of the power of property over the
humble and helpless: a life centered on public service,
rather than private profit. In the United States, he
brought the promise of power and abundance that
would transform life from a painful struggle into a
picnic: everywhere he stood for a release from all con-

strictions, religious, moral, legal, sexual. The disguise
was all the more effective because Caliban had appropri-
ated, from Prospero, the magical spells of science: for
every occasion he could quote a scientific authority, as
the Devil himself reputedly can quote Scripture. Only
recently has it become plain that some of the institutions
we have valued most, some of the changes in the human
personality we have regarded as most beneficent, have
actually abetted the rise of Caliban. Following up this
clue, I purpose therefore to center attention upon two
changes that have come about in the last half-century:
the overthrow of the superego and the domination of
the automaton. Either of these transformations would
have been dangerous by itself: the two together now
constitute a serious threat to our civilization.

The other designation for the "overthrow of the superego" would be the "unchaining of the id." By an un-
usual coincidence, the practical effort was accompanied
by a theoretic explanation; and this explanation first
demands our attention, since it both interprets what has
actually happened and indicates what measures we must
take to overcome the forces of disintegration.

Both the concepts of the id and of the superego, as
essential components of the human personality, were
the outcome of a profound analysis of the human psyche
that has taken place during the last seventy-five years,

178

and very rapidly during the last fifty. The two men who did most to define this change, who added the dimensions of depth and height to the post-theological description of the personality, were two men of contrasting talents and purposes: one of them, Frederic W. H. Meyers, known to his own generation as an investigator of extrasensory phenomena, has been practically forgotten in our time. The other, Dr. Sigmund Freud, stands out as one of the most courageous and original minds that has ever attempted to understand man's nature. The result of these investigations, if I may dare to make such a swift summary, was to establish that the human self is not, to begin with, a simple unity, but a federation of selves, old and new, latent and active, buried and budding.

At bottom, usually below the level of consciousness, is the body and its members and all the processes that go on at an organic level: the instinctual urges and reflex acts, the impulses and promptings and wishes that well up from even deeper strata and reveal themselves enigmatically to us in dreams, or more practically, in proposals and projects that lead to works of art and invention. This primitive underlayer of the self Freud called the id, which is Latin for the aboriginal "it," that which has not yet become "I" or "you" or "we." The id is that part of the spiritual anatomy which Christian theology habitually refers to as the Old Adam; and it is, perhaps, significant that the Old Adam was rediscovered at the end of a century when men blandly supposed that the primitive elements in life had been wiped out by the advance of science and mechanical industry, just as the primitive races were being wiped out—or what was almost the same thing, civilized—by the spread of colonial empires. Like his contemporary, Joseph Conrad, Freud discovered the Heart of Darkness, not just in the African aborigine, but in the soul of modern man himself.

By definition, the id is basic to every other part of the personality. So long as it is attached to the whole personality, as a co-operative member of a federated constitutional government, the id is neither good nor bad. Its undifferentiated and undirected vitality, however, seems as incapable as Caliban's of choosing goals that will even insure its own survival: as Freud pointed out, the id, being the helpless victim of the pleasure principle, has no hold on reality. Indeed, the id in its unmodified state, before it has accepted the discipline of constitutional government, shows many infantile, irrational, even criminal characteristics. We behold the id in its unmodified state in the juvenile delinquent who murders a passing stranger for the pleasure of the experience. Like a little child, it is capable of saying, "I

am going to kill you!" when it only means, "Stop bother-
ing me and go away!" Or Caliban will shout, "You are
a traitor!" when all he means is that the hated creature
holds a different opinion about matters whereon the id,
with its feeble grip on reality, sees no possibility of difference. When it breaks loose from the whole personality the id actually carries out these imbecile threats.

Above the id, Freud uncovered two other layers of
the self, both later than the id, for they are products of
nurture and culture, not just raw nature. One of these
is the ego, the commonplace, conscious, daylight creature, the official presentable self, disciplined by experience to admit that fire burns and ice freezes, no longer
under the infantile illusion of boundless power. The ego
learns to walk warily among other egos, conforming and
compromising, striving for security and status, for recognition and approval, accepting the taboos and customs
and goals of the tribe, performing its appointed social
roles: yet often prompted by the Five Lusts, as the
Chinese call the libido, into seeking channels and expressions of its own, sometimes regressing into the id,
yet sometimes transcending its limitations by creating
an ideal self, masked by a different costume and cos-
metic than that of the tribe. Above the ego Freud detected another aspect of the self, which he called the
superego: the voice of duty and conscience, which seeks

to bring unity into man's often conflicting claims and activities, and to direct them to a purpose beyond his immediate needs and satisfactions.

For Freud, this superego was a sort of universal Mrs. Grundy, and a male Mrs. Grundy at that, for he tended to identify its authority with that of the repressive father, who constantly stood in the way of the male child's incestuous impulses toward his mother; and so deep was his hostility toward his own father, once his eyes had been opened, that he extended to the superego his long-buried resentments. Freud's understanding of this part of the personality was, I regret to say, something less than perfect; for the most patent manifestations of this superego, in its creative aspects, come from the realms of art and religion; and since Freud regarded religion as an outmoded superstition, the product of illusion, he was not in a favorable state to appraise one of its chief characteristics: the fact that, from the age of the pyramid builders onward, it sought to turn man from the limited goal of animal survival to the endless task of self-development, self-transformation, and self-perfection. Though Freud's early disciple, Jung, presently disclosed the mechanism of this development, in his analysis of the prophetic and anticipatory function of the dream, Freud was so obsessed with the notion of the superego as a censor that he actually announced that the object of psychoanalysis was to "strengthen the ego, to make it more independent of the superego." That injunction was dangerous, for it both broke down the unity of the self and challenged the authority of the higher functions.

The reason for Freud's failure of insight here should by now be plain: in his analysis of the development of the self, he left out of account the positive influence of the other member of the family, the mother. Overemphasizing if anything, the rule of the father, the Jovean, power-seeking, repressive, organizing element in the personality, he played down the function of the mother, with her life-bestowing gifts, her relaxing and yielding attitudes, her life-transmitting and life-nurturing functions: the mother's sympathy and responsiveness, her giving of the breast to her infant, her special effort to establish an I-and-thou intimacy through language, her endless ways of expressing love. If one necessary part of the superego is inhibitive and withholding, the other is persuasive and affirmative, expressive and life-enhancing.

Alone either agent, paternal or maternal, may be harmful to the normal development of the personality; for too much mothering, if it lead to overattachment and overprotection, may produce weakness, and that may be as fatal as the harsh commands of an overauthoritarian father. The principle of dynamic balance, so important in all organic functions, holds with particular force here. The superego, to be effective, must draw constantly on the energies of the id at the very moment that, through art, philosophy, and religion, it gives them a creative outlet and a superpersonal goal. If, as Freud thought, art is a mere mechanism of escape, philosophy a rationalization, morality an oppression, religion an outright fraud, the only fragment of the superego left, to counterbalance the id, is scientific truth. How little that leaves us will come out presently.

Now apart from Freud's brilliant theory of dreams and the resulting diagnosis and therapy there was nothing essentially new in this analysis of the self: nothing that was not in large part already familiar to Plato, down to the description of the irrational and potentially antisocial elements that Freud found latent in the id. Did not Zeno the phrenologist discover in Socrates' bumps the evidence of criminal tendencies, and was not Socrates sufficiently well acquainted with himself to admit that these were indeed traits against which he had found it necessary to struggle? But Freud's fresh insight came at a moment when, among the European middle classes, sexuality had been unduly restricted, and in treating neuroses, particularly hysterias, Freud found that the symptoms would often disappear if the patient could be made to confront his or her sexuality and ease avoidable pressures. By lightening the burden of repression, Freud helped to restore order and health in cases where a purely censorious superego had clamped down too hard.

But if sexual repression were the cause of illness, might not the unlimited expression of sexuality be a preventive? That was a tempting thought. Freud himself did not succumb to it; for his own life, as a loving husband and the father of six children, seems a model of domestic felicity, and he turned his own unconscious drive to seek a more sterile goal into an occasion to uncover hitherto hidden areas of the psyche: so that he sublimated his homosexual impulses in science as Whitman did in poetry. But ironically, the popular result of Freud's teaching was to undo the exemplary lesson of his life. The relief of sexual tension widened into a letdown in all tensions: "Be yourself" now came only to mean "Be your lower self." Once the lid was off sex, less attractive components of the id also exploded: cruelty had already found its apologist in Nietzsche, and violence presently found its philosopher in George Sorel. In short, the influence of Freud's teaching, as it was vulgarized, was to favor the id: one of his favorite disciples, Georg Groddeck, even wrote an apologia for the id. With the apparent blessing of science, man's primitive self now rose to the top: it was no longer the body and its members that were despised, but every aspect of the superego, the discipline of morality, the ideal fantasies of art, and above all love. What Dr. Ian Suttie eventually called "the taboo on tenderness" came to characterize both the ideology and the actions of a great part of Western society.

This change did not, of course, take place overnight: still less was it the work of a single thinker. Though Freud was trained in the exacting disciplines of the scientific laboratory, the tendency of his work was to continue the romantic assault on civilization that had been opened in the eighteenth century by Jean Jacques Rousseau. The idealization of the primitive and the spontaneous, the natural and the effortless, was in origin a salutary revolt against life-denying systems of order. The adventurous exploration and settlement of the planet provided a counterpoise to the mechanical routine introduced by capitalism. Vitalities too long held in check by archaic institutions had reason to crave a fresh outlet, if only on a desert island with Robinson Crusoe: hence romanticism had, for a time, an activating and regenerative effect. And this was true, above all, in the political community where nationalism and democracy served as correctives to outworn institutions, molded to protect a single class. But in overthrowing the artificial hierarchies of property and privilege, the twin forces

186

Romanticism and Revolution also tended to turn their back on natural hierarchies: including those that give authority to knowledge over ignorance, to goodness over malice and evil, to the rational over the irrational, to the universal and enduring over the time-serving and particular.

Perhaps the most innocent expression of romanticism occurs in that famous passage in Emerson, in which he justifies his own "departure from the dear old doctrines of the Church in order to 'live wholly from within,' " in the face of the earnest protests of a friend who says: "But these impulses may be from below, not from above." To which Emerson answered calmly: ". . . If I am the Devil's child, I will live then from the Devil." Since Emerson's superego, as the fifth in an unbroken line of clergymen, had been thoroughly formed in the image of God, he had reason to trust in what seemed to him—erroneously, I think—to be a purely individual and spontaneous reaction. But would his serenity have endured had he confronted the works of a real disciple of the Devil, like Himmler or Hitler? The revolt against the superego, which has taken so many forms during the last century, has had the effect of reversing the true order of human development. Primitive and unconscious processes take precedence over rational and conscious ones: hardness and sadism trample on tenderness and

187

love. In short, elements that every high religion has devoted thousands of years to restraining, canalizing, damming, or diverting into distant fields, have now over-flowed every embankment. Yes: the id and the superego have reversed roles. By now it is the primitive urges that give commands, and it is the superego, art and religion, morality and law, that timidly carry out the id's orders.

Do not misunderstand the purport of this analysis. I would not for a moment have you suppose that either Rousseau or Freud, or yet the Romantic poets and novel-ists, by themselves brought about the condition we now face. To hold that view would in itself be to descend to the primitive level of so much current thinking. What is important to grasp is that the result of our increased knowledge of unconscious and primitive urges—the realm of the not-yet-human—has been to besmirch our specifically human qualities, and to lower our faith in human potentialities that transcend past achievements and have still to find their form in new works of art and their incarnation in living persons. The upsurge of the id, in thought and imagination, has given extra energy to a downward movement in world civilization: the forces that should be commanding Caliban are either his helpless victims, or, as so often in modern art and politics, his not unwilling accomplices.

In seeking to understand our primal urges, we have

lost sight of our peculiarly human traits and our potential human destinations, not given in nature but
fabricated and projected by man. How commonplace it
is to reduce every higher human development to a lower
term, the pages of the Kinsey reports reveal with almost disarming—or should I say alarming?—naïveté.
Dr. Kinsey and his associates would regard it as a
ludicrous form of moralism—as it surely would be!—
if we chose to reprove a monkey or a cat for not re-
specting the conventions and sentiments of human mar-
riage. But these seemingly neutral scientists do not
apparently see that it is equally absurd to turn reproof
into justification, in the opposite direction. If animal
behavior justifies sodomy, why not also the murder of
rival males in courtship? If murder, why not cannibalism and incest? Is it not characteristic of this devaluation of the human, that in this whole study of the
sexual life of American men and women, seemingly
so exhaustive, the word love does not appear in the
index of either volume? This is the science of Mickey
Spillanes. By now its one-sided methodology has been
transferred to every human activity: careful of quantities, ignorant about qualities, knowing much about
causes and probabilities but indifferent to purposes.

Had this change in ideas come about during some long
sleepy summer afternoon of Western man's existence,

one might not have noted any general transformation, corresponding to it, in human society. But the traditional manifestations of the superego were theoretically undermined just at the moment when the irrational forces that had been gathering for more than a century had begun to break loose. During this climactic period, the struggle between economic classes had sharpened, and the tension between nations had increased. The resulting conflicts, the strikes, lockouts, assaults, aggressive demonstrations, wars, genocides, broke down long-established inhibitions against violence and spread anger and fear, brutality and terror: presently otherwise normal people were prepared to perform acts against human beings that only a little while earlier they would have hesitated to perform upon live rats. Under wartime conditions, hate and fear and violence are natural responses, indeed psychological accessories to survival. Such conditions pamper and inflate the id, and starve all of man's higher functions. Need I remind you that it is under these negative conditions that mankind has lived for the last forty years: years of hot and cold wars, of ruthless domestic repressions and vengeful revolutions, of widespread municipal gangsterism and fascist sadism, of systematic torture and random extermination. The only self that has been acceptable, under such conditions, is the lower self, hardened to any violence, heavily insulated against reason and love.

During the last forty years few of us have escaped the taint of Caliban: by our passivity, if not by our active connivance, we have contributed to the overthrow of Prospero; indeed, those who should have been most concerned to forestall this debasement have in fact all too often abetted the final betrayal: the real *trahison des clercs*. Because of the set taken by our institutions, we have reached a dead end in human development; and if the infernal instruments supplied by modern science are ever put to extensive use, that may prove a dead end in the most final sense. In descending to the level of the id, we have thrown away every guide and chart wisdom produced in the past to avert this catastrophic conclusion. Our leaders and guides seem as much the victim of their obsessive fantasies of power and retaliation as was Captain Ahab in *Moby Dick:* that mad captain who, when the moment drew near for coming to grips with his mortal enemy, turned a deaf ear to the call of love, uttered by Pip, and cast aside sextant, compass, and chart, only to bring his ship and all but one of its crew to utter destruction. How close to home that symbol now comes! With almost one voice our obsessed and driven leaders in science and government say that there can be no turning back: indeed, no halt or pause for reflection.

In the name of security they go on piling up the weapons that not merely increase our own vulnerability, but that, if used at fullest strength might wipe out the larger part of mankind and perhaps make the whole planet permanently unfit for life. Unlike the physical destructions of World War II, already so largely repaired, we know those of the atomic age will be irretrievable. Yet the only meaning of such a war, if it broke out, would be to relieve the fears produced by the infernal weapons that prompted it: the very process would cancel out every human purpose.

In short, what began as a contempt for the higher functions of life now threatens to end with a contempt for all life; for once men defile their own humanity, life, even if they survive, becomes meaningless, value-less, directionless, death-seeking. By renouncing those emergent qualities that, being attached to the superego, are specifically human, man becomes a monster, finally, even to himself, and an enemy to his own species. Under the irrational and criminal pressures of the id, we have come dangerously near losing even the animal's saving instinct of self-preservation.

But now I come to the final bitter paradox. This revolt of Caliban would hardly have proved so threatening, at least on the scale we now witness, had it not been abetted by another phenomenon: the mechanization of life and the transformation of man, the creator and inventor, into a mere agent of the automaton he has created. Modern man, in revolt against earlier systems of thought, sought to emancipate himself by controlling the forces of nature: by inventing new instruments of power, water mills, gunpowder, coal-burning engines, dynamos, he finally found himself in possession of the cosmic forces locked within the atom itself.

This transformation, which met so fully the id's infantile wish for unrestrained power, was the product of an entirely different sector of the human personality: the detached intellect, freed from all other biological promptings or moral and social claims, pursuing truth with the aid of a new methodology, that of experimental science applied to the piecemeal analysis of the external world. In all matters that lent themselves to quantitative measurement or mathematical proof, this new method produced immense results: above all, a framework of order and with it, an ability to understand, to predict, and in increasing measure to control all natural phenomena. Knowledge, as Bacon had confidently said, was power; and power became the main object of knowledge.

As a result, science became increasingly the only part of the superego that seemed to have objective existence and so was capable of exercising authority. Art and religion became supernumeraries, who danced attendance on their new master in his leisure hours. Unfortunately, this concentration on power, order, knowledge was achieved, both in technics and in science, at the expense of the human personality as a whole. To practice science successfully, its adepts voluntarily submitted to a severe system of restraints and inhibitions: within their own province, they renounced every passion or sentiment or feeling that would interfere with their single end, exact knowledge. The ideal of scientific thought was to be as free from personal bias as if it were the product of a machine. This systematic self-restraint moralized a vast department of thought more effectively than any earlier code of morality: within its own domain it fortified patience, deposed vanity, elevated humility, eliminated selfish bias, enthroned reason. But the personal and social penalty for that achievement was heavy. Causal insight widened, but purposeful direction and creative audacity, in every other department of life, weakened.

With a few admirable exceptions in every period, from Pascal to Clerk Maxwell, the practitioners of science divorced themselves from social responsibility and prophetic anxiety: indeed, they prided themselves on this indifference. The words cold, detached, rigorous, unemotional, in a word, objective, are all considered

laudatory words by the scientist when applied to him.
What does this mean but that science, by its method,
disengaged the scientists from life, from the real world
and the real self in which emotion, imagination, and
dreams are as real as instruments of measurement? Indeed, that in order to concentrate effectively on his own
limited object, the scientist has deliberately fabricated
for himself a defective personality. There is much bi-
ographical evidence to suggest that this very suppression
may itself be the outcome of anxiety, an inability to
face life as a whole, particularly that part of it related
to the scientist's emotional or sexual nature.

But the mischievous results long remained hidden for
the reason that science approaches infallibility in every
department where mathematical analysis, quantitative
measurement, and experimental verification can be applied: thus, in compensation, it gives the devotees a
quiet sense of godlike power. By identifying themselves
with the infallibility and omniscience of science they
escape any sense of their own all-too-human limitations.
Power, order, and knowledge, under these circumstances
become absolutes; not human instruments under human
control. Though the belief in these absolutes is itself the
most dangerous kind of subjectivism, it escapes the
otherwise self-corrective methodology of science. So the
automatic increase of scientific knowledge, technical in-

vention and physical power, has taken on in our time the character of a dangerous neurosis. We have now ruefully to acknowledge that a highly rationalized, disembodied superego is just as incapable of dealing with reality as the primitive id.

The scientist's detachment from life as a whole, his indifference as scientist to any other human values and purposes but his own, explains an otherwise strange phenomenon: the fact that the physical sciences have flourished, the last thirty years, under tyrannous systems of government. Give the scientist freedom to pursue his method, let him preserve his vocational integrity, and he will pursue his researches under social conditions that would be crippling to an artist or a poet or a philosopher. The artist usually cannot work at all under insistent restraint, because he must be a whole man to command his creative processes; if he remains creative it is by heroically pitting all his forces against the regime that thwarts him. But the scientist, who, as a matter of method and principle, turns his back upon the whole man, does not labor under such a handicap: his isolated superego, so highly moralized within its special province, has no need to rebel against less benign forms of repression. If he enjoys the freedom to follow up his researches, the scientist is all too easily lured into serving tyranny, no matter for what base ends his discoveries may be used. Superbly moralized and responsible in his own sphere, he refuses as scientist to acknowledge moral responsibilities outside it.

By our overvaluation of physical power and scientific truth, aloof from other human needs, we have paid the same price Faust had to pay when he made his compact with Mephistopheles: we have lost our souls, or to speak in more psychological terms, we have depersonalized ourselves and have turned our conscious, thinking selves into automatons. Is it any wonder that our whole civilization has begun to behave as if it were under a collective compulsion neurosis: that it goes on repeating processes it has once started, even when they have lost both their original meaning and any valuable humane end? Behold the way in which we continue to produce butter and wheat we neither eat nor share, goods that we do not have the social providence to distribute, knowledge we do not have the intellectual capacity to assimilate, instruments of mass extermination whose use might put an end to the human race.

The scientific superego, so far from helping us to control this relentless automatism, is itself a part of the same process and has no internal means of resisting it. Even the atomic scientists who have been most aware of the dangers issuing from their own discoveries, have never had the insight to question the rationale of their

197

own vocation: rather, with antlike persistence, they have gone on with their researches, consoling their uneasy consciences, perhaps, with the thought that their duty to scientific truth is higher than any other duty to humanity. In repressing the mothering and nurturing impulses in the personality, the scientist has also lost the normal parental concern for the future of the life it cherishes. One hardly knows whether to characterize this attitude as innocence or infantilism; it certainly indicates a failure to reach maturity.

This abdication of responsibility, this failure of forethought, this detachment from all other needs and values than those of knowledge and power, has been one of the contributing factors in the resurgence of barbarism. The only part of the superego to which Freud and his contemporaries unreservedly paid homage—the passion for exact truth—has by its very divorce from the whole personality played back into the hands of Caliban. Detached from the rest of life, the scientific ego becomes automatic; and automatons cannot give provident directions to other automatons. This perhaps explains why, though one part of our culture, that dominated by science and technics, has reached the highest point ever attained in human history, the rest of our existence is falling into planless confusion, directed toward life-negating and irrational goals. These conditions stem from our failure to nurture every part of the human personality, and to match every paternal increase of power with a maternal increase of love, and with a common parental increase of moral control.

Modern man, therefore, now approaches the last act of his tragedy, and I could not, even if I would, conceal its finality or its horror. We have lived to witness the joining, in intimate partnership, of the automaton and the id, the id rising from the lower depths of the unconscious, and the automaton, the machine-like thinker and the man-like machine, wholly detached from other life-maintaining functions and human reactions, descending from the heights of conscious thought. The first force has proved more brutal, when released from the whole personality, than the most savage of beasts; the other force, so impervious to human emotions, human anxieties, human purposes, so committed to answering only the limited range of questions for which its apparatus was originally loaded, that it lacks the saving intelligence to turn off its own compulsive mechanism, even though it is pushing science as well as civilization to its own doom.

It is this last act that we are now beholding in our own time. Those of us who have strong stomachs know the evidential proofs of that union in the records of the Nazi doctors, correctly called Doctors of Infamy, who added a final horror to the Nazi extermination camps. These were men trained in the rigorous impersonal methods of science, who obediently carried through the orders of their superiors in the German government, to perform revolting tortures upon human victims under conditions that counterfeited and hideously caricatured scientific experiments. The detachment of these doctors was admirably scientific: their observations were coldly objective: their indifference to social results was in the best tradition of science—yet their total behavior was depraved. Though that was a classic juncture, revealing depths of evil deeper than any Dante could imagine in his candidates for the Inferno, it is by now a commonplace. But already this partnership has spread far beyond Nazi Germany and Soviet Russia. Is the final purpose of the Nazi crematories in essence different, by any other facts than distance in space and swiftness of operation, from the meaningless extermination of life that would take place in what we now politely call ABC war—a large-scale effort to liquidate the enemy population? Except for omitting the sadistic pleasures of torture, the end that is sought, complete annihilation of the hated object, is precisely the same.

As things are going now, unless a strong countermovement restores our humanity and our sanity, the union of the automaton and the id will probably bring about the catastrophic destruction of our civilization. The godlike powers that scientific thought has opened up to man are now at the service of progressively diabolical means, which have automatically sanctioned equally diabolical purposes. Once set in motion, there is no halting point in that downward descent. The only destination of such a union is the final victory of the irrational: collective genocide and suicide, on a scale that would reduce to meaninglessness the whole process of life's evolution and man's own ascent from brutishness to civilization: leaving that ultimate nothingness out of which only nothing can come.

If I thought that this last act of the tragedy was inevitable, I would not, you may be sure, have consented to give this paper. When a ship is doomed, it is wiser to strike up the band and speak cheerfully to one's fellow passengers than to hold an inquiry over the villains who sabotaged the machinery and planted a time bomb in the hold. But while there is life there is, proverbially, hope. The cries of anger and anxiety that have at last broken through the wall of silence, prompted by the hideous devastations of the hydrogen bomb, were not confined solely to our European and Asiatic friends: the instinct for self-preservation, which could be quieted among us at home when we thought that it was only the Russians who might be endangered by our lethal devices, has at last asserted itself, now that we realize that ourselves and the rest of mankind would be equally stricken, if not completely wiped out, in another large-scale war. What once mistakenly seemed a prudent method of offsetting Russian man power with American atomic power has patently become a gross mockery, now that we ourselves are in even greater jeopardy. This deep anxiety, so much more realistic than the childish assurances with which our leaders have attempted to cover over their radical miscalculations and errors, gives ground for hope: we may yet overcome this coupling of the unrestrained id and the automaton, and redress the balance in favor of life.

Admittedly, the mischief that has already been done will not easily be undone: the genii we have unloosed, as in the Arabian Nights fable, cannot so easily be put back into their bottle. Generations and even centuries may pass before the nightmare that now hangs over man will be finally dissipated; for there remains the possibility that even the peacetime exploitation of atomic energy may bring grave dangers to organic life, before we exercise sufficient restraint. To go forward, we must partly retrace our steps: to overcome the misapplications of power we may be forced, as Christianity was once forced, to give up many desirable applications of technics, in order to have sufficient vitality to nourish other parts of the human personality. We cannot promise ourselves a happy ending or love's final fulfillment in our time. But perhaps, in my next paper, I shall be able to convince you that there are viable human alternatives to the violence and irrationality and hate that now threaten to turn the world first into a madhouse, then into a crematorium. Those in whom, happily, the streams of life yet run freely have still to be heard from. Prospero may yet take command.

IX

THE POWERS OF PROSPERO

In my analysis of the Age of Caliban, the age in which we now live, I sought to dispose, directly and indirectly, of a whole series of facile notions to explain the pathological state in which so many peoples and nations now live: not only our enemies but an active and all-too-influential minority, at least, of our own citizens. The strange thing about this pathological condition is that those who most definitely show its symptoms do not know that they are ill; and even many people who have scarcely been touched by this illness show no sufficient anxiety about the spread of the disease: they are as blandly unaware of the state of our civilization as the ancient Romans, like Symmachus and his circle, who piously believed, at the time the Western Empire was crumbling about their heads, that Rome still had another thousand years to go.

The reason for this strange inertia, this curious mental complacency, has I trust become a little clearer as the result of bringing to light a critical danger and defect in that part of our culture we are most inclined to overvalue: science and technics. The mischief we now face has in part had its origins, I suggested, in institutions and habits of mind that almost all of us have accepted as self-evidently beneficent and on the side of progress, enlightenment, the good life. If knowledge is good, can we have too much of it? If power is good, can we produce it in too great quantities? If mechanical order and automatism are good, why should we keep it from spreading everywhere? For most of our contemporaries these questions admitted only one answer: but the answer they happened to give, that power, knowledge, and order are absolute goods, irrespective of the human use we make of them, irrespective of their destination, happens, as events themselves are at last now teaching us, to be a profoundly erroneous one. We who boast that we are the proud citizens of a free world have been living progressively, for the last two centuries, and more and more for the last fifty years, under repressions and compulsions and automatisms, derived directly from the dominant system of intellectual and industrial production. These automatisms have been as fatal to human development as the more obvious repressions of a more personal kind of absolutism.

If this interpretation seems insufficiently grounded, I must refer you to more extensive analyses I have made in a series of books, beginning with *Technics and*

Civilization and ending with *The Conduct of Life:* inquiries that parallel those made in philosophy by Whitehead, Jaspers, and Northrop, in the philosophy of history by Henry Adams, Schweitzer, Toynbee, Sorokin, and Ortega y Gasset. Almost a century ago isolated observers were aware, beneath the sleek varnish of Victorian humanitarianism and optimism, that the new barbarian invasion was gathering its forces within Western society: Delacroix, Dostoevski, Burckhardt, de Tocqueville, all made shrewd prognoses. During the last half-century, both Henry Adams and H. G. Wells characterized the crisis of our time as a race between education and catastrophe. The continued rise of Caliban is essentially a witness of the failure of education. But behind that lies a deeper failure, due partly to our misplaced faith in the absolutism of science: a failure to understand the nature of the modern world, the nature of human society and the human self, and finally, a failure to perfect the disciplines that would reintegrate the severed parts of the human personality and encourage a more fruitful and benign development.

Now a disease that has so long been insidiously fastening itself on the organism cannot in all probability be thrown off quickly: indeed, even if there were a philosophical or theological wonder drug at hand—and I personally know of no such agent—we would probably find, as physicians do with similar therapeutics in medicine, that the period of convalescence is nevertheless a long and trying one, with mischances of its own that demand watchful attention. We have allowed the untutored and unconditioned id, the raw primitive, to become detached from the whole self and we allow its utterances to displace the voice of reason and the promptings of love.

Similarly, we have allowed an overdeveloped organ of human intelligence, equally detached from the whole personality, to divert to its own uses the energies that belong to the entire superego. Pursuing the power to control nature, we have lost the wisdom and will necessary to control ourselves, and we thus become helpless cogs in the mechanism we ourselves have created. The impersonal processes of science lead to the treatment of dynamic, self-impelled subjects as mere objects, of persons as things, and to a systematic disregard of the claims and aspirations of the whole personality, from which science itself, incidentally, has issued. By treating this depersonalized existence as if it alone were the real one, we have created a new world, a world of mechanical collectives and individual automatons in which only automatons have the full status as citizens, since by the rules that govern this world every human quality, apart from those that serve the pure intellect, is a defect, or at worst, a superfluity and an extravagance.

In such a world, it becomes easy to conceive of exterminating a million people in a city by a hydrogen bomb, as if they were a million rats in a garbage dump: for when human values and purposes disappear, human beings themselves become vermin to each other, and finally, by contempt for the law of their own nature, become vermin, likewise, to themselves—the lousy victims, as they might put it, of a lousy civilization.

This whole process has been exquisitely summed up in a personal letter to me from Roderick Seidenberg, the author of *Post-Historic Man;* and since it arrived at the moment when I was trying to make my own summation, I will, with his permission, quote it to you, instead of succumbing, out of envy, to the insidious temptation to paraphrase these thoughts more clumsily in order to conceal my debt to him. "Your plea in The Times," he writes, "brings to my mind an idea which haunts me: each culture evolves a characteristic bodily posture or gesture that symbolizes its essential values; thus Christianity brings to mind a suppliant figure on its knees in prayer; the Buddha sits in the calm of eternity with snails in his hair! The gods and Pharaohs of Egypt are seated—great granite figures of power. There is in these postures an element of the ultimate, an expression of a transcendent attitude. But what, pray, is our posture

upon having miraculously touched the innermost sources
of nature's power? Our school children here in the back-
woods of the village of Tinicum are taught in daily drill
to duck under their desks when they hear the siren blow.
The citizenry have built themselves deep underground
shelters where they are to cower while their civilization
is blown to atoms. And those not fortunate enough to
grovel in fear and trembling underground are taught to
fall upon their faces in the gutters of their cities and
await their doom. Prostrate, our heads deep in the mud,
we face the future! Such is our posture."

I hesitate to mar those words with a single further
comment: but does not Mr. Seidenberg's analysis reveal
the real posture of our civilization and properly deflate
the paranoid pride that leads us from one irrational act
to another even more fatal one? We have fallen victims,
in our mind at least, to a temptation strangely like the
temptation faced by Jesus of Nazareth. We have been
led to the top of a high mountain and shown how we
might rule all the kingdoms of the world, on one simple
condition—that we use the cosmic power at our command to destroy them entirely, and in the very act of
consummating that destruction, give our own empty
selves to the Destroyer. Is it not time that we retraced
our steps quickly, down from those dizzy heights, and
asked ourselves under what terms we may become

human again? Plainly it is not by increasing our power
but by redeeming our humanity that we shall be saved.

Let us begin then by reconsidering the nature of man:
he who is more than an animal yet less than a god. Part
of the self-understanding we need, that which has to do
with man's biological and social past and with all the
repetitive processes in which his life is involved, we
shall gratefully draw from the findings of science, re-
assured rather than upset by the fact that the nearer we
come to the core of man's nature, as described in an-
thropology and psychology, in history and biography,
the more we find the method itself infected with subjectivity, until, at the very recesses of man's innerness
—in the heart of the secret and undisclosable I—he becomes inaccessible to any directly verifiable observation, and thereby escapes from the confident statistical
determinism of science.

To understand man's nature, we must look for it at
every level: in his biological functions and needs, in
his psychological dispositions and wishes, in his social
claims and commitments, and finally in his religious
strivings and aspirations: that is to say, we must look
for that nature both in his biological and his cultural
past and in his ideal or projected future. But to account
for man's whole nature, we must include in his history a
time element that, since Aristotle, has played no part

210

in scientific calculations: the sphere of the potential and the possible, the sphere of his real creativity. Many of man's present actions have meaning only in terms of an ideal self or an ideal destination to which, throughout recorded history, he has, with increasing clarity of purpose, been groping. If man builds for his God a more magnificent building than he thinks proper for his daily self, it is because God, in all his historic forms and postures, symbolizes the utmost conceivable potentiality: power transformed into omnipotence, time extended into eternity, life transposed into immortality, love overcoming all antagonism and separation. Without grasping this inner disposition toward transcendence, man's daily behavior cannot be fully and competently interpreted: for there is no stimulus in his crude environment, not even the spectacle of the sun and the stars, that is capable of evoking such a response: the movements of the planets stand for necessity, not human and divine potentiality. Other animals fulfill their nature by being true to the fixed mode of their species: man fulfills his nature by being true to his latent possibilities, and by making his own future.

What man has learned in the past about his own nature, as expressed in the religion, the morality, and the art of the higher cultures, from the early dawn of conscience in Egypt onward, must now be rediscovered and set in a new framework, joining with present-day knowledge that vastly amplifies it and at many points fully confirms it. Much that man, for instance, has discovered in biology about his close organic partnership with other living species, and further about his constant dependence upon and co-operation with all forms of life, re-enforces with empirical observations the intuition of a Buddha or a St. Francis. This interpretation not merely puts man's estate in evolutionary perspective: it likewise explains why this creature, all stuccoed over with reptiles, as Walt Whitman so well put it, is subject to so many humiliations, so many bumfalls and backslidings, when his mounting pride causes him to forget his lowly animal origins.

Certainly modern man must acknowledge his place in the animal world, realizing, since Darwin, that even his emotions and sentiments, not least love and loyalty, have their beginning in the behavior of his mammalian progenitors. But he must also accept the fact that his intelligence and skill have made him the dominant member of this world. Though he himself cannot exist without the constant co-operation of other forms of life, down to the lowliest bacteria, he must in turn accept his role as an over-all guardian of life, responsible for maintaining an ecological balance that replaces the automatic controls of nature. Unless he preserves the rev-

erence for life inculcated by every religion, he may
undermine his own existence, indeed bring it to an end.

All this is important: but it is only part of the
knowledge and self-understanding modern man needs.
For there is another side to this process that has largely
been either ignored or misinterpreted: the process of
ascent and emergence, which by its very nature goes
beyond the point where science, with its causal method,
can allow itself to go. Inevitably, science tends to explain more highly developed forms in terms of the less
highly developed ones, the last step in the process by
the succession of steps that led up to it: indeed all causal
explanation is retrospective, and its success in prediction
is due to its being confined to past observation of regularities and repetitions.

In causal explanation, the donkey—if I may put an
old figure to a new use—moves only because of an
external stimulus, the whip applied at the rear, not
because he seeks the carrot in front. Still less has causal-
ity any notion that in man, if not in the donkey, the
carrot that produces this action may at first be a subjective projection or an illusion, and yet turn out, in
the end, to be as effectual as the whip and capable of
bringing forth real carrots by the bushel. Fully to account for man's behavior, particularly to understand its
prospective reference, one must invoke the principle of

teleology, or purposive action toward an imagined and projected end. In such a development the conceived future controls present actions and adds value and significance to immediate satisfactions by attaching them to larger fulfillments in which other men share. So, too, the complex final state throws a light on the earlier events that led up to it: indeed the significant pattern, the emergent value, becomes fully realized—and fully visible—only in the last stage. To take in man's nature, in other words, one must not merely examine his origins but understand his goals—not least those ultimate goals which, like the distant summit of Everest, are barely discernible from the highest platform where man has yet camped.

There have been many definitions of man; and I should hesitate to add still another were it not for the fact that most of our modern definitions seem to me to overlook the heart of the matter. I would define a man as the unfinished animal, the radically dissatisfied and maladjusted animal who comes up with a thousand different answers to each of Nature's proposals. Man is the only animal who is not content to remain in the original state of nature. That sense of being unfinished, alterable, transformable, perfectible—and yet, by a negative process likewise deformable, degradable—is the very essence of the human condition. We, who are so

used to considering man's nature in terms of the indig-
nities that are heaped upon it, or of the many varieties
of vileness and demoralization that it discloses in a disintegrating world, might well go back to Pico della
Mirandola's essay *On the Dignity of Man* to get a
sounder view of human nature.

"God," observes Pico, "took man as a creature of
indeterminate nature and, assigning him a place in the
middle of the world, addressed him thus: 'Neither fixed
abode nor a form that is thine alone nor any function
peculiar to thyself have we given thee, Adam; to the
end that according to thy longing and according to thy
judgement thou mayest have and possess what abode,
what form, and what functions thou thyself shalt desire.
The nature of all other things is limited and constrained
within the bounds of laws prescribed by us. Thou, constrained by no limits . . . shalt ordain for thyself the
limits of thy nature. . . . As the maker and molder
of thyself, thou mayest fashion thyself in whatever
shape thou shalt prefer. Thou shalt have the power to
degenerate into lower forms of life, which are brutish.
Thou shalt have the power, out of thy soul and judgement, to be reborn into the higher forms, which are
divine.' "

Note the part of wishes and claims, longings and
aspirations, in this definition of man. Not merely does

215

man choose and seek goals not indicated by his original constitution, but he remains, to his glory, as permanently dissatisfied with the self he achieves as he is with the original state of brute nature. Not only man's life but at bottom all life seems to show teleological characteristics: it is formative, directional, goal-seeking; but in the kind of self-transformation that has been at work in the evolution of organic species, both the purpose and the goal have been so closely built into the process that we are flatly at loss for suitable terms, not painfully anthropomorphic, to describe what goes on. Let us take a homely example from the Museum of Natural History. To suggest that an insect that looks like a walking twig came into existence by a series of accidental variations in its germ plasm that cumulatively brought about its deceptive twiglike form is to make accident itself a more incredible miracle worker than any theologian's Providence; while to suppose, as alternative, that an originally untwiglike insect experienced a platonic desire to become like a twig and contrived that laborious transformation so that he might in this disguise safely continue his career as an insect, seems in causal terms hilariously funny.

Perhaps it would be less insulting to our intelligence to assume that purpose and form are as aboriginal and irreducible as mass and motion: that purposeful transformation is in fact another term for life and must be included with such other attributes as irritability, self-maintenance and reproduction. At all events, when we reach man, the evidence reads more plainly: in him the given organism with its blind instinctual drives is supplemented by conscious purposes that push him beyond his purely animal state. Truly, as Pico says, he is a maker and molder. Everything he touches, tools, machines, landscapes, cities, artifacts of all kinds, laws, codes, patterns of conduct, bear the stamp of human purpose. By art, his inner wishes are materialized, and by thought his material circumstances, in a reverse process, become etherealized, as A. J. Toynbee would say. Transposed into ideas, these spiritual forms become in turn the starting point for a new cycle of materialization. Yet all these projects, plans, proposals have in the end a single goal: man's own self-transformation. The more far-reaching and many-sided the transformation, the fuller and richer the life.

The prime instrument of man's special kind of emergent purposefulness has been in process of improvement over a vast evolutionary cycle: the central nervous system. All the automatic processes in man's body, the hormones, the sympathetic nervous system, the reflexes, have the function of taking care of the life-maintaining processes, without conscious intervention, so that great amounts of psychic energy can be concentrated in the evaluating, integrating, decision-making center. This surplus of energy, a surplus visibly recorded in man's excess of brain capacity and unused neurones, has resulted in an increase in feeling, an increase in sensitivity, an increase in the capacity to dream and symbolize and project; and all these qualitative changes amplify in every direction the otherwise narrow utilitarian role of man's intelligence. Without the free play of his imagination and invention, man's life would have been as repetitive as the life of insect societies, like the ants: fixed in the same mold for at least sixty million years. Out of an original exuberance, an overflow of sounds, images, spontaneous movements, anticipatory dreams, welling spontaneously from within, man was able to mold a new self and along with it a self-sustaining culture. Had man been content with the animal role of adaptation and conformity, he would never have produced language or symbolic thought, religion or art or science. Yet man's highest work of art is neither a poem nor a symphony, neither a mathematical equation nor a city: his highest work of art is himself. Perhaps only once or twice in a generation is the ideal self of a culture incarnated in a living person: a Sophocles for Greece, a Dante for medieval Italy, a Milton for England, a Goethe for Germany, an Emerson for New England; yet it is toward that end that every other process and function is directed. When man ceases to toil at that art, he abandons his main lifework: sometimes as in our own day, he covers over that self-betrayal by plunging himself desperately into external activities, planning trips to the moon or journeys through space in a desperate effort to get away from himself and to forget all his buried possibilities.

If what I am saying makes sense, we are now close to the point of understanding how the depersonalization of man which has gone on during the last century has had the effect of crippling him and has made it increasingly difficult for him to participate in activities more meaningful than those the automaton itself provides. No part of man's life has value, except in terms of the person and the community he is in process of actualizing and realizing. The very essence of human character, indeed of morality itself, is purposeful action in terms of an ever-emerging and ever-enlarging whole. In that process one may have to sacrifice a lower possibility for a higher one, a temporary good for a durable good: but when no goal or purpose exists, other than that of keeping the machine running, if, indeed, from the standpoint of the machine the person himself is expendable, the very temptation to be human disappears. At that point Caliban's career seems as attractive as Prospero's.

No amount of material success can give such a civilization a substitute for a valuable and purposeful life. In short, we must face the fact that the classic religions have always clearly indicated: without the effort to achieve a higher life, to seek, as the saying is, the Kingdom of Heaven, nothing that can properly be called human life is possible; though a culture may carry on for centuries on the momentum acquired in some earlier effort. When man lives for purposes beyond his limited self or his generation, beyond those of his group or his tribe, these universal purposes command subjective energies comparable to those within the atom: at such moments, only at such moments, man attains to his utmost creativity. At that last stage, energy is at the service of vitality, vitality at the service of humanity, and humanity at the service of divinity. To establish that chain of command, we must address ourselves, first of all, to our ultimate goals. While our highest aspirations and purposes are still fragile, in comparison with our biological needs, they are not, in fact, any less imperative.

Almost from the first breath of life, the higher expressions of the spirit are essential to man's normal development. Human values and sentiments seem to play a part like that of the vitamins and the trace elements in diet: they must be present, if even the lower elements are to perform their function. I have, I confess, once

220

before been reproved by a somewhat supercilious academic authority for using this metaphor; but I use it again, with a cheerful grin in his direction, because it seems to me singularly accurate, and because it helps to account for the tendency of a more gross kind of psychological appraisal to overlook the importance of apparently insignificant activities and delicate fitful stimuli, like looking at a pair of courting birds in spring or pausing at night, as Emerson usually did, to take in the starry sky.

No human being can live for very long, in a normal state, without enjoying a modicum of meaning, value, and purpose, of fellow feeling, friendliness, affection, and love. Even the simplest bodily appetites need, in order to prosper at all, the extra sustenance of love and hope. When they are present one can live on in an iron lung; and when they are gone the world itself becomes little better than an iron lung. Infants brought up in an orphanage languish on the same diet that would make a child who had received love robust and animated. In a hospital I know of, a bright, efficient immaculate place, visitors used to see a slovenly old woman, who wore no uniform, shuffling along the corridors, crooning tenderly with a baby in her arms. When questioned about her, the doctors would explain that, when one of their infants was seriously ill, and seemed to do poorly under normal nursing practices, they had learned to turn the little patient over to this old crone, and she would often, by the magic of her body and her love, bring the child back to life. Love, and the responses that love gives, are essential for human development. If nothing that can be called the higher life can be imagined without drawing on the resources of the id, the reverse is equally true: the instinctual self, for its own security, must be coupled to the superego: otherwise the id is self-annihilating, death-seeking.

From all this it follows that every attempt to transfer authority from the whole man to some fraction of him —even such a high and significant fraction as that represented by scientific thought—is an aberration and a practical perversion. It is by understanding man's whole nature and by fostering constant intercourse between various parts that his balance can be maintained, and his normal growth and development assured. This doctrine saves us from two equally unfortunate distortions. One was the mistake first made by the classic religions and then repeated in another form by modern science: that of letting the highest elements in the organic hierarchy, man's inhibiting and directing propensities, exercise a tyrannical authority over the rest of the self, in the interests of a disembodied spirituality or an equally detached rationality. Such a tyrannous and unloving

superego sooner or later brings about the revolt and re-
venge of Caliban. Those who would oppose reason to
emotion, as if the first guaranteed integrity and the
second would overthrow it, have learned little about
the nature of the human personality. Herbert Spencer's
wise remark, that it is as possible to be debauched by
work as by idleness, applies to every part of the self:
the sin never lies in the offending member, but in its
separation from the other members, and from the higher
purpose they serve through their union. It is separation
that gives the id a disproportionate influence, and this
applies equally to the superego. Many a saint has lived
to regret his mistreatment of his body. Did not Francis
of Assisi repent, at the end of his life, that he had been
so unkind to Brother Ass, as he called his body, and did
not Ignatius Loyola, a more wary psychologist, guard
his novices against too severe mortifications of the body?
But life itself quickly redresses this kind of error:
medieval culture, which placed a high value on chastity
and virginity, produced, as Chaucer smilingly reminds
us, the Wife of Bath.

But today, on the contrary, our overemphasis and distortion comes from the opposite direction; and unfortunately, nature has provided no automatic method of
compensation. We in America overwhelm the higher
functions by constant and never-ending insistence upon

the lower ones, just as we will interrupt the music of Bach or Mozart to advertise a cigarette or a laxative. Our life has become an air-conditioned nightmare: packed with sensations and emptied of purposes, glutted with things and starved of meanings; or rather, we attempt to derive all our meanings and values from the world of dehumanized objects, and, in the ideal case, allow ourselves no subjective interest that matter or motion, in one of their popular forms, would not satisfy. Kinesthesia followed by anesthesia sums up the current formula for the good life.

Both morally and politically, accordingly, we fail in self-government: we have simply developed no selves sufficiently disciplined to control our agents and instruments. Odd fragments of the personality intrude erratically, like spirit voices in a séance, giving contradictory directions for our daily activities: the religious self, the scientific self, the practical self, the national or tribal self, the domestic self, the mean sensual self, do not form a working federation, under a responsible person. Indeed, the whole apparatus of advertising, publicity and political propaganda, so characteristic of modern culture, is dedicated to the end of undermining a stable centralized inner authority, capable of making real choice. Instead, all too often, the masses of men are tempted to submit to the decisions of an external author-

ity—a dictator, a grand Lama, or a Cybernetic substitute
—who arrogates to himself this normal human responsibility.

Are we not all more or less in the plight of that
pathetic Marine colonel, who to explain his submission
to his Communist inquisitors, said, in so many words,
that the effect of their methods was just like that of
American advertising: namely, to deprive him of choice.
What a giveaway that was of both modes of conditioning! Let us not deceive ourselves by our glib habit of
making a black-and-white contrast between the totalitarian and the free world. Though we Americans cherish
a Constitution and a system of law designed to protect
the person and safeguard his freedom, too large an area
of our life has become compulsive and automatic: too
much of our existence operates without benefit of intelligence, by mere routine, without moral restraint,
without reference to a humane scale of values, without
a further purpose, indeed, than to make the machine go
faster and faster. This applies to every part of our
productive system from motorcars to hydrogen bombs.
The soul of man has become a shriveled mummy secreted
in a narrow inner chamber of an enormous pyramid:
the very size of the tomb reveals the littleness of the
spirit within it.

This brings me back once more to the nature of man.

We have failed to understand the forces that threaten our existence, because the dominant philosophy of life —the pragmatic philosophy upon which everyone habitually acts—has failed to do justice to man's condition and his unique character. By cutting off the superego, and deliberately mutilating a good part of it, modern man has blocked the path of his own development. In pursuit of objectivity and certainty, we have elevated the object and depressed the subject: that is, our very selves. This means, we have depleted man's faith in his own creativity and in his relation to those inner forces that prompt man to project a destiny for himself not given directly by external nature or by his own animal or historical past. By treating religion and morality as if they were illusions, we have succumbed to the most childish of illusions: that man can protect himself against malice and mischance, against evil and perversity, without concerning himself with the meaning of existence and without seeking a higher goal than mere survival. On the way back to reality we will have to reverse this process: instead of freezing our feelings, emotions, values, wishes, dreams, we must utilize them deliberately, under a more comprehensive personal control: self-confident, self-reliant, self-directing.

Unless we are prepared, then, at every moment to consider the nature and the destiny of man, unless we realize that he has little reason for existence except as the vehicle of an ideal self and an ideal future that transcends this existence, we cannot be trusted with the cosmic powers that are now in our possession, indeed we will only stultify and defeat ourselves with much smaller powers. Though these convictions are deeply embedded in every classic religion, they are not to be identified with any single revelation: indeed the existing cults and creeds in the West have all-too-plainly suffered the same erosions and corruptions as the rest of Western society. In the face of much greater threats than colonial domination, no general awakening comparable to that promoted by Gandhi in India has yet swept over our civilization: the voice of an Albert Schweitzer, summoning us to reverence for all life, still has the hollow sound of a voice uttered in an empty hall. How, indeed, can we do reverence to life if we have forgotten half its manifestations, in ourselves: if we grovel before the image of Caliban, and if we turn our backs to Prospero, denying the reality of ideals and depriving ourselves of the ability to give ideal forms to realities?

What I am saying comes finally to this: we will not summon the political will and intelligence to control the powers that we have unleashed outside us, unless we develop the potentialities that exist within us, and project new goals that lie beyond us. Neither the release of the id nor the extension of the province of the scientific automaton are a prudent response to the situation man now faces: or rather, both of them, if uncorrected by the intervention of the feeling, evaluating, loving, life-directing elements in the personality, will probably bring the whole long effort of human history to a catastrophic close, like that foretold in the Norse myth of Ragnarok: the end of the world, marked by the conquest of the gods by the giants.

At this point, I might well leave you to your own solemn thoughts were it not for the fact that such an abrupt ending would probably awaken in you a sense of grievance and in me one of frustration. For I am as much aware as you are that Prospero is still an outcast on a lonely island, and that Caliban, who has long since kept Prospero confined to his narrow cell, is not merely still unchained and rampant, but has worshipers who would ply his drunken ego with more powerful intoxicants. You may fail to see the connection between the broad generalizations I have been making about the nature of man and the concrete ends and duties of the day: the confinement of Caliban, the restoration of Prospero. Sooner or later, you will be driven to ask: What do we do now?

To answer you in detail, even if the spirit were willing, I would have to give a whole course of lectures on the renewal of life, the control of the automaton, the culture of the balanced man, the rebuilding of the super-ego; and each one of these would have to be rounded out with a program and a discipline that you could apply, personally and in groups, to the ordering of your daily activities. That would be a formidable task, and it would take a better man than I am even to outline it in a fashion I should consider adequate. As for its actual translation into a whole way of life, that is something that will doubtless take generations, if not centuries, even supposing that mankind awakens in time to avert the catastrophes that our irrational pursuit of power has prepared for us. Let me reduce that gigantic burden to a little bundle more suitable to my strength, and conclude with a few practical maxims, that may at least point in the right direction. By an exercise of charity you will close your ears to the mumblings of an elderly Polonius, and remember only the occasional flash of Prospero.

And to begin with, the control of Caliban. The first place in which to confront this monster is in oneself; and the first measure involves nothing more or less than an act of faith: a belief in the ability to exercise control. Do not, under the delusion that you are being objective or scientific, blot out the distinction between higher and lower, good and bad, feeling and unfeeling, intelligent and automatic, purposeful and random, both within your own nature and within every province that it touches. Repressing Caliban is not simply a negative matter: it is made easier by giving energy to the life-enhancing functions, by every manner of ordered and purposeful expression. As Emerson approvingly said, when pianos were first sent to raw pioneer settlements: *"The more piano the less wolf."* Never favor the lower functions at the expense of the higher, except when it is necessary to restore balance and equilibrium: never give vent to purely instinctual drives except under the providence of the whole self. This means that anger must be tied to the sense of justice, that orgasms must be at the service of love, that intellectual curiosity must be attached to social responsibility, that the will to power must be curbed by the desire for social approval and the obligation of service.

What applies to the discipline of the individual applies in a greater rather than a lesser degree to the conduct of a nation; for every individual vice and blemish is magnified a million times in the collective ego. One must not, out of pride, speak of one's nation in terms that sane, self-respecting men would never apply to their individual selves; and similarly no nation must, out of fear, take steps for its self-preservation which would remove the moral basis for that self-preservation. You and I may kill in extremity in self-defense; but if we want to live with ourselves afterward, we must not torture in self-defense, nor kill as a preventive measure, to rid ourselves of anxiety. So, too, we may shoot a criminal resisting arrest, if we are armed with the authority of law: on those terms, under the auspices of the United Nations, our country lawfully and morally helped resist Communist aggression in Korea: an act to implement justice and ensure peace.

But one must not shoot every member of a criminal's family as a way of ensuring the criminal's prompt surrender to an agent of the law: our pleas for using wholesale genocide, in a retaliatory action against an aggressive totalitarian government, would be of that order. How can we hope, as a people, to rebuild the normal human personality, and create a humane and peaceful world, as long as we publicly commit ourselves to preparation for the total extermination of our enemies: such a division between Dr. Jekyll, the healer, and Mr. Hyde, the killer, is internally disruptive. Even if absolute justice were on our side—and that is far from being true—the method would by itself defeat the ends of that justice: namely, to establish a world in which men of good will can live in brotherhood and peace. The public renunciation of the methodology of barbarism to which we have unthinkingly committed

231

ourselves is the first step toward sanity and by itself would be a contribution to comity and confidence between the nations. So much for the prime effort to overcome the inner demoralization that delivers us into the hands of Caliban.

As for the control of the automaton, that lends itself to no simple measures: it is a matter, in the personal realm, of keeping strict guard over one's habits, for that is where automatism actually begins, and of intervening even in the practice of good habits, lest they become compulsive, and so out of control, and so finally indifferent or hostile to life's needs. My own rule here is to reduce membership in all organizations where personal acquaintance and personal intercourse is impossible, where the I-and-Thou relation has been destroyed and a system of remote control initiated; and when I am a part of such an organization, as I certainly am as a professor in a big university, I seek, at least in my own province, to break or challenge the automatisms that come from above. Only by keeping a wary eye on one's freedom and retaining the initiative can one safely use all the automatic processes that actually simplify and lighten the physical burden of life. If we begin by letting the process control the product, we end by letting the product control the producer. None of us should be so wedded to security and smooth routine that we could not dare to yank the lever and stop the whole works, in order to regain the human initiative. The failure of our scientists to understand this fact betrayed even those who had a sufficient moral conscience to feel troubled. In fact, the more pervasive and beneficent the automatic process, the more need there is then to establish a multitude of small centers of control and to build up whole areas that are immune even to a benign invasion. That, and not escapist rocket flights into outer space, is one of the big jobs of the coming century.

Now we come to the proper domain of Prospero: the domain in which control and direction, inhibition and expression, evaluation and discrimination should increase in proportion to the energies and vitalities that they command. The first demand of this part of life is to orient oneself, not by immediate landmarks, but by the abstract points of the compass; and to correct one's watch, not by reference to other local clocks, but by reference to astronomical time, as established by the world's observatories. This brings one back, as to a base line, to the great prophets and sages of history; for though they have not said the last word about man's life and destiny, any scheme of life today that departs widely—and on the basis of a few generations of observation and experiment—from the standards set up by the classic religions and translated into daily disciplines and rituals over many centuries is likely to overlook important human needs, and what is quite as important as these needs, deep human aspirations.

Hinduism, Buddhism, Confucianism, Hellenism, Hebraism, Islam, Christianity, all differ in various ways as to their interpretation of the ultimate mysteries of life and the cosmos: but they are equally concerned with the ultimate context, the overshadowing purposes and ends that polarize all the lesser activities and functions of man. The scientific knowledge of our time richly supplements these insights and in many cases re-enforces and expands them. We have reasonable expectations, for example, through our deepened insight into human psychology, of being able to achieve more effective self-discipline and self-education. Some of the goals of religion have been as difficult to achieve, without this scientific support, as the dream of flight was impossible before science and technics had supplied the necessary data and means. There was more than a touch of truth in Samuel Butler's jibe that as an instrument of morality Christianity is only a flint implement. But science, by definition, has no organ of prophetic anxiety and prophetic foresight, no place in its methodology for dream and form and ideal; and without all these attributes, so far best embodied in religion and art, a fully human life cannot be lived. Only those so fortified by a larger, self-transforming purpose are capable of overcoming the irrationality and violence of our time.

The domain of Prospero is the province of religion, morality, and art, and every part of that province must be freshly cultivated if we are to overcome the forces that now threaten us. In many departments, we must plow under the weeds and tares that have infested these fields; for a complacent religion, whose values and transformations are all in the past, is no religion; a conventional morality, which accepts all the idols of the tribe, is no morality; and an art that has become both formalized and formless is no art. But to make these domains important again, we must apply ourselves to them, with all the energies we command, and give them hours that are now drained away by joyless recreation, infantile hobbies, and mindless work. Against the shallow vocationalism of our day we must oppose the great vocation of Man, the vocation of becoming more fully human, and of supplanting each achieved self with a higher and more universal self.

Each of us must ask himself: What portion of my life do I spend in the service of an idea and a purpose that will outlast this life and at the same time greatly fulfill it? If we answer these questions frankly, confessing our grudging services or our total evasions, we shall realize why Prospero's powers have dwindled steadily in our time. For most of us a small period of our lives is given, usually under compulsion, to the service of the State: but how little of our lives in these United States is given to the more positive purposes of the community, even to the extent of serving on public committees and boards. And how much less is given to more universal forms of service and remoter purposes! Yet those in our time who have risen to such larger purposes wholeheartedly —whether in war or in relief service after the war— count such years among the best years of their lives, though they were often accompanied by hardships and deprivations of the severest kind. In a new fellowship of service they found a fulfillment that their peacetime lives had lacked. And it is the lack of such goals in Western culture that has driven, and continues to drive, so many people into the service of bastard religions, like fascism, nazism, or communism, which, by simulating many of the characteristics that a transcendent religion shows in its period of growth, have demonstrated their power to release energy and to promote a selfless yet utterly self-fulfilling devotion. You cannot, as the G.I. in Korea remarked, oppose Marxism with Coca-Cola. Only a more universal religion, capable of enlisting a great dedication, can overcome the attraction of Caliban masquerading in the garments of Prospero. Democracy will prevail only when it overcomes its obsession with na-

236

tional sovereignty and national power: when it projects a greater and more universal vision of life than any existing state incorporates. Where ego was, to paraphrase Freud, there superego shall be. This applies equally to the ego of the individual and the collective ego of the group or institution: the tribe, the city, the church, the nation. Whereas in the past, the struggle for survival divided mankind into exclusive and mutually repellant groups, the necessities for survival now demand that they overcome this suicidal isolationism.

Where the tribe and state were, there shall a united mankind be. The beginnings of that transformation have already been made in our day; but for lack of energetic faith they have been diverted and halted. We have yet to understand that our armaments give feeble protection, compared with such acts of mutual aid and nurture as the UNRRA and the Marshall Plan and the United Nations itself. All of these works have now to be translated into more permanent forms, which will equalize wealth and cultural opportunity among the nations of the world, just as the income tax, in countries like England and the United States, has, as a matter of common justice, begun to equalize them within these countries. Under the command of a reborn superego, we shall direct our lives so that we may offer gifts of love to neighbors we shall never see and serve children who are not yet born. This providential rebirth of the super-ego, this recapture of human potentiality, is the budding life wish of our time: the only means of opposing and counteracting the death wish that now has at its command forces capable of universal destruction.

And finally, there is one great realm of Prospero that must be redeemed from those who have usurped it, and opened up for those who are ready to cultivate it: the domain of love. The only final safeguard against the genocidal and suicidal impulses our weapons of extermination have encouraged, is the sedulous devotion to love in all its aspects, beginning with tenderness. Each of us, all of us, must cultivate tenderness within ourselves, and be as committed to nonviolence as Mahatma Gandhi, as loath to wipe out the life of the most insignificant fellow creature as a devout Jain, knowing that all life is precious, even the humble life of a Japanese fisherman, yes, feeling the deepest repugnance against the wanton contamination or extermination of the fish he seeks to catch for food. We will have lived to some purpose if we are tender enough to earn Caliban's contemptuous characterization of us as the "hand-wringer" or the "bleeding heart." Let our hearts bleed freely as long as a single human being suffers from preventable misery or rectifiable injustice. Yes, and let us stanch that blood by effective remedial action, whether the sufferer lies on our doorstep or waits for succor on the other side of the earth.

Here I would apply, further, doubtless in the manner of Polonius, a little of the country wisdom I have come by; for I have found over the years, as a father, that the more one looks after an infant, the more paternal and loving one's attitude becomes: almost as with the old James-Lange theory of the emotions, the behavior itself helps to produce the appropriate response. Just as the domestication of animals domesticated man as well as the sheep and the ox, so the sedulous nurturing of life brings a special reward to the physician and the teacher as well as the parent. By accepting responsibility for a single life we increase our capacity for love: by accepting responsibility for all life, we would not merely deepen the foundations of love, but make all other men the beneficiaries of that security, releasing them from hatred as well as fear. I regret I have no time to spell out all the practical consequences of this reorientation, but it has an immediate political application.

Again, I have found that when I give my neighbor some of the surplus vegetables in my Dutchess County garden, I feel a glow of love promoted by the very act of giving; and he in turn feels the same way, when I receive his gifts; indeed, he may even be a little reluctant to receive with grace unless my own attitude is

239

equally responsive. This give-and-take is the very dialogue of love; and it is different from an equitable commercial transaction for the reason that the gift must be freely given, without thought of reward, and just as freely reciprocated, without thought of calculated repayment. As a country, we are so far from following the ways of love that we have almost forgotten these conditions; our fellow citizens feel aggrieved, too often, because after we have given away billions of dollars, our friends in other countries still do not love us and do not reciprocate by doing the things we held secretly to be part of the bargain. But love is love: it is neither rape nor prostitution: "The gift is to the giver," as Whitman said, "and comes back most to him." In the long run, love begets love as surely as hate begets only hate.

This self-transforming and self-transcending quality of love cannot be called upon for all the little occasions of life, when customary civility and politeness must do duty instead. Part of its magic arises from its freedom and spontaneity, its sudden sense of the occasion, its ability to depart from the expected routine. But when love is genuine, it has the power to open doors that would remain locked and bolted against forceful entry. All over the world, power divorced from love has become insolent, brutal, irrational, and increasingly manic and paranoid; and by those very attributes has become impotent and self-defeating. Now that power has over-reached itself, love offers the only alternative that will lead us back to life: the Sermon on the Mount has thus become the new Mount Everest that calls forth the human spirit today. Nothing less than that "impossible" ascent remains as a practical alternative to our yielding to the destructive and inhuman forces that threaten our whole civilization. That is the last word of Prospero.

ACKNOWLEDGMENTS

I "In the Name of Sanity" was first published in *Common Cause*, January, 1950; and is here printed in a shortened version.

II "Assumptions and Predictions" first appeared in *Air Affairs*, March, 1947, under the title "Social Effects of Atomic Energy."

III "Technics and the Future of Western Civilization" was presented at the Hundredth Anniversary of the American Association for the Advancement of Science in September, 1948.

IV " 'Miracle' or Catastrophe" first appeared in *Air Affairs*, July, 1948. Part of it was used in "Alternatives to the H-Bomb," in *The New Leader*, June 28, 1954.

V "Mirrors of Violence" was first printed under the head, "Mirror of a Violent Half Century," in the *New York Times Book Review*, January 15, 1950.

VI "Renewal in the Arts" was one of a series of lectures given at the University of Pennsylvania in April, 1950, under the title "From Revolt to Renewal," and was first printed in *The Arts in Renewal*, University of Pennsylvania Press, 1951.

VII "Irrational Elements in Art and Politics" was presented at the Corcoran Gallery in Washington, D. C., January, 1954, under the auspices of the Institute of Contemporary Arts and the Phillips Gallery, and was first printed in the *New Republic*, April 5 and 12, 1954.

243

ACKNOWLEDGMENTS

VIII and IX   "The Uprising of Caliban" and "The Powers of Prospero" were given in a slightly shorter version at the Brooklyn College (The Franklin Matchette Foundation Lectures) on May 3 and 4, 1954. The first lecture was published in the summer, 1954, number of the *Virginia Quarterly Review*.

To the various editors and sponsors of these essays and lectures, I give my warm thanks for their encouragement and, perhaps I should add, their courage; as well as for their permission to make this further use of my work.